First Workshop on Speech-Centric Natural Language Processing (SCNLP 2017)

Copenhagen, Denmark
7 September 2017

ISBN: 978-1-5108-4762-0

Printed from e-media with permission by:

Curran Associates, Inc.
57 Morehouse Lane
Red Hook, NY 12571

Some format issues inherent in the e-media version may also appear in this print version.

Copyright© (2017) by the Association for Computational Linguistics
All rights reserved.

Printed by Curran Associates, Inc. (2017)

For permission requests, please contact the Association for Computational Linguistics
at the address below.

Association for Computational Linguistics
209 N. Eighth Street
Stroudsburg, Pennsylvania 18360

Phone: 1-570-476-8006
Fax: 1-570-476-0860

acl@aclweb.org

Additional copies of this publication are available from:

Curran Associates, Inc.
57 Morehouse Lane
Red Hook, NY 12571 USA
Phone: 845-758-0400
Fax: 845-758-2633
Email: curran@proceedings.com
Web: www.proceedings.com

EMNLP 2017

The First Workshop on
Speech-Centric Natural Language Processing

Proceedings of the Workshop

September 7, 2017
Copenhagen, Denmark

©2017 The Association for Computational Linguistics

Introduction

The first Workshop on Speech-Centric Natural Language Processing (SCNLP 2017) took place on Thursday, September 7, 2017 in Copenhagen, Denmark, immediately preceding the Conference on Empirical Methods in Natural Language Processing (EMNLP).

The purpose of this workshop was to unite the automatic speech recognition (ASR) and natural language processing (NLP) communities to discuss new frameworks for exploiting the rich information present in the speech signal to improve the capabilities of natural language processing applications. Our community objective is to revisit the conventional NLP problems with a focus on incorporating the richness of spoken language, as well as to encourage research contributions that promote cross-fertilization between statistical methods for ASR and NLP.

Our inaugural workshop was held at EMNLP to encourage participation amongst the NLP community to consider and discuss the challenges of combining speech recognition with conventional NLP research, as well as to appreciate the recent successes in this exciting field. The authors in these proceedings have combined ASR and NLP in works that address part-of-speech tagging, constituency parsing and dependency parsing on speech, information extraction and spoken term detection, dialog state tracking and speech translation, as well as two research assessments that evaluate the fluency and adequacy of English speakers and the role of speech silence in conversational dialogs.

The invited talk was given by Gabriel Skantze, entitled "Modelling turn-taking in spoken interaction."

Our workshop also contained an open round-table discussion about the current state of speech-centric NLP and some of the research and pragmatic issues that raise a barrier of entry for the larger research community.

We would like to thank the members of the Program Committee for their reviews, as well as our panelists who led our round-table discussion. We also would like to thank the authors for their contributions.

Nicholas Ruiz and Srinivas Bangalore
Co-organizers

Organizers:

Nicholas Ruiz, Interactions (USA)
Srinivas Bangalore, Interactions (USA)

Program Committee:

Francisco Casacuberta, Universitat Politècnica de València (Spain)
Eric Fosler-Lussier, The Ohio State University (USA)
Dilek Hakkani-Tür, Google (USA)
Xiaodong He, Microsoft Research (USA)
Peter Heeman, Oregon Health & Science University (USA)
Julia Hirschberg, Columbia University (USA)
Preethi Jyothi, IIT Bombay (India)
Gakuto Kurata, IBM Research, Tokyo (Japan)
Lin-shan Lee, National Taiwan University
Yang Liu, University of Texas at Dallas (USA)
Karen Livescu, Toyota Technological Institute at Chicago (USA)
Raymond Mooney, University of Texas at Austin (USA)
Satoshi Nakamura, Nara Institute of Science and Technology (Japan)
Mari Ostendorf, University of Washington (USA)
Giuseppe Riccardi, University of Trento (Italy)
Andrew Rosenberg, IBM T.J. Watson Research Center (USA)
Isabel Trancoso, Laboratòrio de Sistemas de Lingua Falada (Portugal)
Jason Williams, Microsoft Research (USA)

Invited Speaker:

Gabriel Skantze, KTH Royal Institute of Technology (Sweden)

Table of Contents

Conference Program

September 7, 2017

8:50–9:00   *Opening Remarks*
Nicholas Ruiz and Srinivas Bangalore

9:00–10:00   Invited Talk

9:00–10:00   *Modelling turn-taking in spoken interaction*
Gabriel Skantze

10:00–10:30   Session I

Functions of Silences towards Information Flow in Spoken Conversation
Shammur Absar Chowdhury, Evgeny Stepanov, Morena Danieli and Giuseppe Riccardi

10:30–11:00   *Coffee Break*

11:00–12:30   Session II

Encoding Word Confusion Networks with Recurrent Neural Networks for Dialog State Tracking
Glorianna Jagfeld and Ngoc Thang Vu

Analyzing Human and Machine Performance In Resolving Ambiguous Spoken Sentences
Hussein Ghaly and Michael Mandel

Parsing transcripts of speech
Andrew Caines, Michael McCarthy and Paula Buttery

Enriching ASR Lattices with POS Tags for Dependency Parsing
Moritz Stiefel and Ngoc Thang Vu

12:30–14:00   *Lunch*

14:00–15:30 Session III

End-to-End Information Extraction without Token-Level Supervision
Rasmus Berg Palm, Dirk Hovy, Florian Laws and Ole Winther

Spoken Term Discovery for Language Documentation using Translations
Antonios Anastasopoulos, Sameer Bansal, David Chiang, Sharon Goldwater and Adam Lopez

Amharic-English Speech Translation in Tourism Domain
Michael Melese, Laurent Besacier and Million Meshesha

Speech- and Text-driven Features for Automated Scoring of English Speaking Tasks
Anastassia Loukina, Nitin Madnani and Aoife Cahill

15:30–16:00 *Coffee Break / Poster Discussion*

16:00–16:25 Session IV

Improving coreference resolution with automatically predicted prosodic information
Ina Roesiger, Sabrina Stehwien, Arndt Riester and Ngoc Thang Vu

16:25–17:50 Round-table: Issues in Speech-centric NLP

17:50–18:00 *Closing*

Functions of Silences towards Information Flow
in Spoken Conversation

Shammur Absar Chowdhury and **Evgeny A. Stepanov** and **Morena Danieli**
and **Giuseppe Riccardi**
Signals and Interactive Systems Lab
Department of Information Engineering and Computer Science
University of Trento, Italy

Abstract

Silence is an integral part of the most frequent turn-taking phenomena in spoken conversations. Silence is sized and placed within the conversation flow and it is coordinated by the speakers along with the other speech acts. The objective of this analytical study is twofold: to explore the functions of silence with duration of one second and above, towards information flow in a dyadic conversation utilizing the sequences of dialog acts present in the turns surrounding the silence itself; and to design a feature space useful for clustering the silences using a hierarchical concept formation algorithm. The resulting clusters are manually grouped into functional categories based on their similarities. It is observed that the silence plays an important role in response preparation, also can indicate speakers' hesitation or indecisiveness. It is also observed that sometimes long silences can be used deliberately to get a forced response from another speaker thus making silence a multi-functional and an important catalyst towards information flow.

1 Introduction

Silence is a multifaceted natural phenomenon in human conversations that carries information rich in meaning and function. Even though "silence" is generally defined as the absence of speech (Jaworski, 1993) or a break in a conversation flow, its occurrence has the power to deliver a message, as well as trigger human response similar to any other conversational behavior. Silence in human conversations provides insights into the thought process, emotion, and attitude (Richmond et al.,

1991) among others. At the same time, silence is used to convey power (dominance) (Saunders, 1985; Tannen, 1990), respect, and manage conflicts.

Along with speech, silence is an integral part of human interaction, and the two complement and provide information about each other. In the words of Bruneau (Bruneau, 1973):

"Silence is to speech as the white of this paper is to this print"
– Thomas J Bruneau.

Given that the reasons for silence are limitless, it also has many functions. One function is "eloquent silences" that includes the use of silence in the funeral, at religious ceremonies, as a legal privilege, or in response to a rhetorical question (Ephratt, 2008). Apart from this, silence can be used to indicate topic avoidance, lack of information to provide response, agreement, disagreement, anger, frustration, uncertainty, hesitancy and others.

Over the years, researchers have studied silence with respect to, but are not limited to, the location of silence in a conversation (Richmond et al., 1991; Jensen, 1973) or its role in a conversation (Cappella, 1980; Zimmermann and West, 1996; McLaughlin and Cody, 1982) or how its duration changes with different emotions (Alam et al., 2016). Silence has also been studied as a method for non-verbal communication (Kogure, 2007; Bruneau, 2008) and its practices in different cultures (Richmond et al., 1991), or in different contexts. It has also been observed as a powerful tool for conflict-management (Oduro-Frimpong, 2007), and within the context of psychotherapy (Frankel et al., 2006; Gale and Sanchez, 2005; Ladany et al., 2004; Ronningstam, 2006).

Unlike research on speech, the studies on silence are either definitional (theoretical) or de-

Proceedings of the First Workshop on Speech-Centric Natural Language Processing, pages 1–9
Copenhagen, Denmark, September 7–11, 2017. ©2017 Association for Computational Linguistics

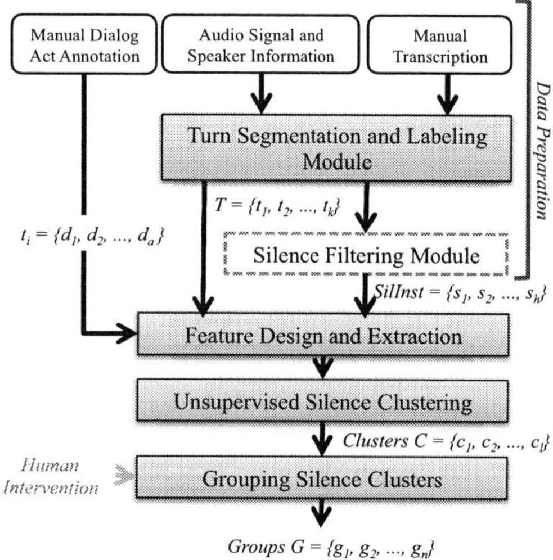

Figure 1: Framework for categorizing functions of long silences.

scriptive. Even within speech research communities, there are very few studies that have analyzed function of silence in a methodological manner. Generally, in a dialog system, silence is not acknowledged as a form of interaction, but rather its function in a conversation is seen as a "pause" or a "gap". Whereas speech is viewed as the primary carrier of information. Thus, a further study of silence and its functions is important, as silence *often does serve as a message,* or at least as *means that offers contextual cues to the surrounding speech.*

Therefore, the goal of this paper is to analyze the function of long silences[1] occurring between and within speakers in dyadic spoken conversations. Our focus is on understanding the perceived reasons of such functions towards the information flow in spoken conversations.

The paper is organized as follows. An overview of the experimental methodology used in this study is given in Section 2. We present an analysis of our findings in Section 3 and provide conclusions in Section 4.

2 Methodology

The methodology followed for grouping functions of the long silences is shown in Figure 1. The pipeline includes a data preparation phase, which involves extraction and selection of the long silence instances; followed by the feature design and

---

[1]In our study, we defined long silences as having the duration greater and equal to 1 second.

extraction phase. The next phase in the pipeline is unsupervised clustering of the selected silence instances, which are later grouped into hierarchical clusters for the analysis of their functions.

2.1 Data Preparation

For this study, we have used conversations from the SISL Human-Human Conversational Discourse Corpus. The data is a subset of a large Italian call-center corpus where call center agents are engaged in conversations with real customers. The customers are calling to solve some specific problem or seek information. The inbound Italian phone conversations are recorded on two separate audio channels with a quality of 16 bits, 8kHz sample rate. The collected conversations ($\approx 10K$) have an average duration of 396.6 ± 197.9 seconds.

To analyze the role of silence in information flow of the conversation, we have selected 10 conversations that contain manual dialog act annotations (Chowdhury et al., 2016b) following dialog Act Markup Language (DiAML) (Bunt et al., 2010, 2012) annotation scheme. The details of the dimensions and the communicative functions considered for the annotation are given in Table 1. The dimensions such as: Discourse Structuring, Speech and Turn Management dimensions are mapped to the tag *Other*, as they are very infrequent.

2.1.1 Extraction of Silence

Silence positions, as well as turn types, such as speakers' turns, overlapping turns, are extracted using the *turn segmentation and labeling system* (Chowdhury et al., 2016a). The input to the system is the audio of the conversation, the manual transcription and speaker information.

The forced-aligned transcription is obtained using an in-domain Automatic Speech Recognition (ASR) (Chowdhury et al., 2014). Lexical information from these forced-aligned transcripts is used to extract turn-taking sequences. The pipeline uses the time aligned output as tokens to create Inter-Pausal Units (IPUs) for each input channel. IPUs are defined as segments of consecutive tokens with no less that 50 ms gaps in-between. Using the time information of inter-IPUs and intra-IPUs, we then define **steady conversation segments** where each segment maintains a steady time-line for both interlocutor channels. The labels of each silence segment are then defined by a set of rules as follows:

- Pause (P): Gaps between the turns of the same speaker with no less than 0.5 second. P_A and P_C represent agent and customer's pauses respectively.

- Lapse between speakers (L_B): Floor switches between the speakers with a silence duration of 2 seconds or more.

- Lapse within speaker (L_W): Gaps between the same speakers' turns with a silence duration of 2 seconds or more.

- Switch (SS): Floor switches between the speakers with silence duration of less than 2 seconds or with overlapping frames not more than 20 ms. This category is also know as *gaps*.

The labeled turn sequences are then used to select silence instances for the analysis.

2.1.2 Silence Filtering

From the 10 conversations we have extracted 433 instances of silences with the duration greater or equal to 1 second. The instances are categorized into two groups:

- Between-Speaker Silences (B): These instances of silence include gaps between different speaker turns that are greater or equals to 1 second. $B = \{S_l, L_B\}$, where S_l stands for gaps $>= 1$ second and < 2 seconds where as L_B are lapse between speakers $>= 2$ seconds.

- Within-Speaker Silences (W): These instances of silence include pauses between the same speaker's turns that are greater or equals to 1 second. $W = \{P_l, L_W\}$, where P_l stands for pauses $>= 1$ second and < 2 seconds where as L_W are lapse within speaker $>= 2$ seconds.

For the initial analysis, the instances of long silences that occur after or before overlapping speech (61 silence instances) are ignored. As a result, the analysis is performed on 372 instances.

2.2 Feature Design and Extraction

Even though silence is an inherently valueless phenomena that possesses no function on its own, individual instances of silence gain its meaning and function from the surrounding context. Consequently, modeling functions of silences requires conceptualization of the context and features that capture it. Dialog acts carry specific communicative functions such as question, answer, expression of agreement, disagreement, etc. Since dialog acts are assigned to the speech segments (turns) that surround the long silences, they provide the information that could be used to model the context of silence instances.

Table 1: Core dimensions and communicative functions from ISO 24617-2 standard considered for dialog act annotation.

Dimension	Comm.Function	Group
General (Task)	*Information Transfer Functions*	
	Question Set Question Choice Question Propositional Question Check Question	Information Seeking
	Inform Answer Confirm Disconfirm Agreement Disagreement Correction	Information Providing
	Action Discussion Functions	
	Offer Promise Address Request Accept Request Decline Request Address Suggest Accept Suggest Decline Suggest	Commissives
	Suggest Request Instruct Address Offer Accept Offer Decline Offer	Directives
Time Management	Stalling, Pausing	
Auto-Feedback	Positive, Negative	
Allo-Feedback	Positive, Negative, Feedback Elicitation	
Social Obligations Management	Initial-Greeting, Return-Greeting Initial-Self-Intro, Return-Self-Intro Apology, Accept-Apology Thanking, Accept-Thanking Initial-Goodbye, Return-Goodbye	

The dialog act dimensions and communicative functions listed in Table 1 are used as features for the analysis of between and within speaker silence instances. Each turn preceding or following a silence is transformed into a feature vector using one-hot representation for dialog acts.

The vectors encode information such as the following. Feedback, a joined dimension of auto-feedback and allo-feedback, (fb) = $\{0, 1\}$, where $fb=0$ represent the absence of feedback dialog acts in the turn and vice-versa. Similarly, the vector also includes other dialog act dimensions like Time Management (tm), and Social Obligations Management (s). The General dimension is split into two: (a) information seeking (q) and (b) information providing and action discussion functions

(ac). The motivation behind such a split is to distinguish between information seeking dialog acts which impose an expected pattern on its recipient, i.e an obligation to provide the requested information.

Since according to the DiaML annotation standard a turn can contain several dialog acts, the vector representation specifically encodes the last dialog act of the preceding turn ($lact$) and the first dialog act of the turn following the long silence ($fact$). Both $lact$ and $fact \in \chi$, where as $\chi = \{$Ac, Q, F, TimeM, Ap, Thank, Int, Other, None$\}$. In the set, χ, Ac represents communicative functions from *information providing and action discussion* functions; Q represents *Information Seeking* functions; F represents *Feedback (auto-feedback and allo-feedback)* functions; Apo represents *apology and accept-apology* functions; *Thank* represents *thanking and accept-thanking*; *Int* represents *initial and return greetings, self-introductions, and goodbyes*; *Other* represents all the dialog acts not used for the analysis. *None*, on the other hand, indicates absence of dialog acts.

The feature vectors of preceding, pr ($|pr|$=6) turn, and succeeding (following), su ($|su|$=6) turn, are merged to represent a silence instance for categorization ($|sil| = 6 * 2 = 12$).

2.3 Unsupervised Annotation of Silence Function

The described representation of silence instances is applied for clustering using Cobweb clustering algorithm (Fisher, 1987) – a well-known concept formation system designed to model human concept learning. Cobweb constructs clusters using "concept hierarchy" that optimally and incrementally accounts for the observed regularities on a set of instances. In other words, given a set of silence instances, Cobweb discovers a classification scheme that covers the patterns with respect to provided feature vectors. Instead of forming concepts at a single level of abstraction, Cobweb groups instances into a classification tree where leaves represent similar instances, and internal nodes represent broad concepts. The generality of a broader concept increases as the nodes approach the root of the tree. Each cluster is characterized with a probabilistic description.

The classification tree is constructed incrementally inserting the instances into the tree one by one. When adding an instance, the algorithm traverses the tree top-down starting from the root of the tree. At each node, there are four possible operations: (a) insert (b) create (c) merge and (d) split. These operations are selected with respect to the highest category utility (CU) metric (Gluck and Corter, 1985). The metric is derived from the categorization studies in cognitive psychology and is shown in Equation 1.

Category utility, CU, attempts to maximize both (a) the probability of the instances in the same category to have feature values in common; and (b) the probability of the instances in different categories to have different feature values.

$$CU(C_l) = \sum_i \sum_j (Pr[f_i = v_{ij}|C_l]^2 - Pr[f_i = v_{ij}]^2) \quad (1)$$

In the equation, $Pr[f_i = v_{ij}]$ represents the marginal probability that feature f_i has value v_{ij}, whereas $Pr[f_i = v_{ij}|C_l]$ represents the conditional probability that feature f_i has value v_{ij}, given the instance belongs in cluster C_l. $CU(C_l)$ estimates the quality of individual cluster.

To measure the quality of overall clustering of the silences, we calculate the average category utility function $CU(C_1, C_2, .., C_k)$, as shown in Equation 2.

$$CU(C_1, C_2, .., C_k) = \frac{1}{k}(\sum_l Pr[C_l]) \quad (2)$$

In the equation, k is the total number of categories. The overfitting is controlled by $\frac{1}{k}$.

Therefore, for each set (B,W), we applied Cobweb clustering algorithm implemented in (Hall et al., 2009) with acuity $A = 1.0$ and cutoff threshold of $C = 0.0028$.

3 Analysis

3.1 Resulting Clusters

For between-speakers silences (B), we have obtained 24 leave clusters, whereas for within-speaker silences (W), we have obtained 26 leave clusters. The distribution of dialog act sequences in each cluster is given in Tables 2 and 3.

3.2 Categorization of Silence Functions

Assuming that each cluster represents a specific function of a silence, the clusters are manually grouped with respect to their parents in the classification tree. The manual grouping of silence clusters is performed considering conversation scenarios surrounding the silence events. For instance,

Table 2: Preceding (column two) and succeeding (column three) turn communicative function sequences for each clusters and their frequency inside parenthesis for between speaker silences. The first column of the table represents the classification tree's leaf id of the corresponding cluster.

Id	Preceding turn dialog acts	Succeeding turn dialog acts
2	question(19); checkquestion(9); inform question(2); inform checkquestion(2); inform autopositive question(1); choicequestion(1); autopositive checkquestion(1)	answer(12); confirm(11); inform(3); answer inform(3); disconfirm(2); confirm inform(2); disconfirm answer(1); answer request(1)
3	question(2); initialselfintroduction initialgreeting returnselfintroduction question(1); initialselfintroduction initialgreeting initialselfintroduction question(1); inform checkquestion(1); choicequestion(1)	other(2); autopositive(2); autopositive returngreeting stalling inform(1); allopositive(1)
5	question(2)	stalling answer(2)
6	question(1)	stalling checkquestion(1)
8	initialgreeting initialselfintroduction question(2)	returngreeting returnselfintroduction answer inform(1); returngreeting inform(1)
9	initialselfintroduction question(1)	returngreeting returnselfintroduction(1)
11	inform(20); request(6); confirm(2); answer(2); suggest(1); stalling request(1); offer(1); initialgreeting initialselfintroduction request(1); inform none inform(1); answer request(1); answer autopositive inform(1); agreement(1); addressrequest(1)	inform(22); acceptrequest inform(4); inform inform(3); confirm(3); acceptrequest(2); inform question(1); answer request(1); agreement(1); addressrequest(1); acceptoffer inform stalling(1)
13	autopositive(16); allopositive(1)	inform(15); inform request(1); correction(1)
15	other(6)	inform(5); suggest(1)
17	answer thanking(1)	inform(1)
18	pausing(2); stalling(1); inform stalling(1)	inform(2); confirm(1); answer(1)
19	allopositive none(1)	inform inform(1)
22	inform(23); answer(2); request(1); correction(1); confirm(1); acceptrequest inform(1)	autopositive(19); autopositive inform(4); autopositive question(3); autopositive checkquestion(2); allopositive(1)
25	allopositive(1)	autopositive(1)
29	pausing(1)	autopositive(1)
31	inform(10); answer(4); confirm(3); request(1); disconfirm(1); correction(1)	question(12); checkquestion(6); question inform(1); question checkquestion(1)
33	autopositive(2)	question(2)
34	autopositive(1)	question acceptthanking(1)
37	inform(2); confirm(2); offer(1)	pausing(4); stalling(1)
38	inform(1)	none(1)
43	other(5)	other(5)
45	other(1)	returnselfintroduction(1)
46	initialgreeting initialselfintroduction question other(1)	returngreeting(1)
47	inform(2); request(1); other inform(1); declinerequest(1); answer(1); acceptrequest(1)	other(5); other stalling(1); other other question(1)

Table 3: Preceding (column two) and succeeding (column three) turn communicative function sequences for each clusters and their frequency inside parenthesis for within speakers silences. The first column of the table represents the classification tree's leaf id of the corresponding cluster.

Id	Preceding turn dialog acts	Succeeding turn dialog acts
2	inform(95); answer(6); request(3); stalling inform(2); inform inform(2); correction(2); question request(1); offer(1); inform request(1); confirm(1)	inform(90); request(5); answer(5); inform inform(4); offer(2); inform stalling(2); inform question(2); suggest(1); inform stalling inform stalling(1); correction(1); addressrequest(1)
3	none(1)	inform(1)
7	pausing(2)	question(1); checkquestion(1)
8	autopositive(1)	question(1)
9	question(8); checkquestion(3); inform question(1)	question(8); checkquestion(3); question inform(1)
10	question(1)	other(1)
11	question(1)	pausing(1)
12	question(1)	autopositive autopositive(1)
14	other(1)	apology inform(1)
15	other(3)	other(3)
16	other(1)	autopositive inform(1)
19	pausing(1)	pausing(1)
20	inform stalling(1)	stalling(1)
21	autopositive pausing(1)	pausing autopositive inform(1)
22	stalling(1)	other inform(1)
23	autopositive(1)	other(1)
24	autopositive(5); autopositive autopositive(1)	autopositive(4); autopositive thanking(1); autopositive question(1)
25	autopositive(1)	stalling inform(1)
29	inform none(1)	none inform(1)
33	stalling(1); pausing(1); other stalling(1)	inform(3)
34	autopositive(5)	inform(4); inform autopositive question(1)
36	question(4)	inform(3); inform inform(1)
37	other(1)	inform(1)
39	inform(9)	stalling inform(7); stalling(2)
40	inform(7)	question(4); question inform(2); choicequestion(1)
41	inform(2); agreement Null inform(1)	autopositive(3)

in a conversation a participant may expect an answer to a question or a contribution from another speaker that might yield a long silence due to the time required to prepare an answer. It might take long to get the information to the query or simply be an act of noncompliance. This long silence period is considered as a failure to contribute to an ongoing conversation. To repair this speakers may use strategies such as repeating the query, changing the topic, or ask for more time to respond.

Below we give example scenarios observed in the silence cluster groups:

The Between-Speaker Silence cluster groups are:

- A mode of response preparation (RP): In this group, there can be two subcategories based on the type of response given by the speaker after the silence. The subcategories are:

  - Response to the previous turn's question in the form of information that includes an answer to the question, a feedback, or asking for more time to answer. This category includes clusters **RP1**=$\{2, 3, 5, 6, 8, 9\}$.

  - A response can also be a question to the information/feedback provided in the previous turn. This category includes clusters **RP2**=$\{31, 33, 34\}$.

- A mode of information flow (IF): These silences can either be a: 1) conversational silences where both speakers are exchanging information or feedback 2) forced silences (deliberate[2]), where the current speaker is using a silence as a tool to force the interlocutor to respond. The member clusters of this group are **IF**=$\{11, 13, 15, 17, 18, 19, 22, 25, 29, 37, 38\}$.

- Silences in Other categories ($B - Oth$): These are the silences which are motivated by factors, such as discourse structuring, not considered in the study. This group includes clusters

---

[2]These silence instances are usually longer. For this study the threshold for this type of silences is $>= 2$ seconds.

B-Oth=$\{43, 45, 46, 47\}$.

The above-mentioned categories are presented in Examples 1 and 2. In Example 1, we observe that the caller is asking the call center operator a reason behind an action, and the act is followed by a long silence of 1.41 seconds. After the interval, the operator is passing some information regarding the earlier query by the caller. From the operational point of view, the interval might have been used to either acquire information or to structure it. Similarly, in $RP2$ scenario in Example 1, after the operator informs that the 'electric power' will not be activated, the caller is taking a long silence of 1.38 seconds to respond to the given information, asking another question. This silence could have been again used for preparing the answer, or it might be the time taken by the responding speaker to compose the next action. In Example 2, we present a scenario where the silence category IF is used deliberately to force another speaker to reply.

The silence in both examples may play other cognitive functions such as controlling emotional attitudes. However, as the focus of this study is to understand the function of long silences in the information flow, these cognitive functions are not considered.

Example 1. **Example of silence category** $RP : RP1$

```
caller: al distacco perfetto ora eh eh
        su che base mi perdoni
caller: the complete interruption ... perfect! now
        ehm ehm due to what reason, excuse me?
        (1.14) Category - RP1
operator: ah ascolti qui ci sono una
          serie di fatture malgrado
operator: Listen (please) we have here a number of
          unpaied bill in spite of
```
Example of silence category $RP : RP2$
```
operator: la luce non gliela riprist
          non viene ripristinata
operator: the electric power will not be reactiv will
          not be reactivated
          (1.38) Category - RP2
caller: ma cosa devo pagare se io ho
        gi conguagliato tutto con
        trecentoquarantacinque euro mi
        perdoni cosa devo pagare la
caller: but what do I have to pay if I have already
        paid 345 euros I beg you pardon but what do I
        need to pay the
```

Example 2. **Example of silence category** IF
```
caller:    [lei deve fare una cosina
           lei ha un delle]
caller:    [You have to do a small thing you have
           some]
operator:    [per e se]
operator:    [but and if]
```

```
caller: belle schermate a disposizione
        mi deve aprire la mia ehe il mio
        fax inviato il ventitr zero otto
        duemiladodici cortesemente
caller: beautiful screens available you have to open
        my own and you will find my fax sent on 23rd of
        August 2016
        (2.12) Category - IF (deliberate
        silence)
operator: vediamo subito
operator: let us see immediately
```

The Within-Speaker Silence cluster groups are:

- Organizational silence (CS): The long pause used for the purpose of organizing the information flow in the conversation This group contains clusters of silences where a speaker is providing information and the silence between turns can either be a time taken to think, find information, or to compose and plan the next turn. **CS**=$\{2, 3, 19, 20, 21, 22, 23, 24, 25, 29, 33, 34, 39\}$.

- Indecision or Hesitation silence (H): In this groups of silences, speaker is either confused about some information, needs clarification, or have some queries. The member clusters of this groups are **H**=$\{7, 8, 9, 10, 11, 12, 36, 40\}$.

- Silences in Other categories ($W - Oth$): These are the silences which are motivated by other factors, not considered for the present study. This group includes clusters **W-Oth**=$\{14, 15, 16, 37, 41\}$.

Example 3. **Example of silence category** CS **and** H
```
caller: non riesco a parl devo
        parlarle ho parlato con cinque
        suoi colleghi e mi hanno
        chiamato due consulenti
caller: I cannot tal ... I need to talk ... I talked with
        five colleagues of you and two consultants called
        me
        (1.16) Category - CS
caller: io oggi pomeriggio devo andare
        dall avvocato per denunziarvi
        per diecimila euro al giorno di
        danni che mi avete arrecato da
        stamattina
caller: this afternoon I will go my lawyer for
        sueing you due to ten thousand euros in damage
        per day due to this morning (power) interruption
        (1.65) Category - CS
caller: ehe perch io ho gi pagato
        tutto nel
caller: ehm because I already paid all what I due
caller: senso che tutte queste
        bollette sono state conguagliate
        con una di
        trecentoquarantacinque euro
        incluso
```

```
caller: because all these bills were paied with
        another one of 345 euros including
caller: il mese di luglio e agosto
caller: the months of July and August (as well)
        (1.57) Category - CS
caller: ehe avevo gi chiarito il (.)
        primo distacco l abbiamo sospeso
        mi hanno richiamato perch non
        trovate una vostra lettera di
        risposta
caller: and I already told this when (.) there was the
        first interruption (that) was suspended they
        called me because you are not able to find a
        reply letter from you
        (1.01) Category - H
caller: ora devo (.) parlare con lei o
        devo parlare con qualcuno sopra
        di lei mi perdoni se sono
        abbastanza
caller: now (I) have (.) to call with you or have (I)
        to call with you boss? sorry but (I) am enough
```

In Example 3, we present dialog scenarios with assigned categories. It is observed that the top three long silence intervals are used either to plan the next turn or to take the time to think. Whereas in the last (shortest) silence of 1.01 second, before threatening the operator, the caller either hesitates, feels bad, or is not sure whether a threat is going to work.

The duration distribution statistics for each category of silence functions are presented in Tables 4 and 5. For between-speaker silence categories, in Table 4, it is observed that median duration of silence category $RP2$ along with $B-Oth$ are longer compared to $RP1$ and IF. As for within-speaker silence categories, it is observed that median duration of H categories is longer than CS. The observation is explained as the speakers might need more time to take the next turn when s/he is facing indecision, hesitation, or need clarification about something.

Table 4: Statistics of between-speaker long silences categories.

Between-Speaker Silence	RP1	RP2	IF	B-Oth
1st Quadrant	1.21	1.33	1.27	1.36
Median	1.37	1.76	1.59	1.96
3rd Quadrant	1.62	2.67	2.13	2.93
No. Instances	47	23	107	12
Total	189			

4 Conclusion

The main focus of this analytical study is to explore the functions of long silence within and between speakers towards the information flow in a conversation. In an attempt to find such functions, the study utilizes the sequences of dialog act tags

Table 5: Statistics of within-speaker long silences categories.

Within-Speaker Silence	CS	H	W-Oth
1st Quadrant	1.13	1.10	1.32
Median	1.36	1.42	1.63
3rd Quadrant	1.76	2.63	2.06
No. Instances	145	29	9
Total	183		

present in the left and right context (concerning speaker turns) surrounding the silence itself, and designs feature vector to represent a long silence. These designed feature vectors are later used to cluster silences using a well-known hierarchical concept formation system (Cobweb), which is designed to model different aspects of human concept learning. Following the clustering, we have manually grouped the clusters into functional categories and have studied their significance, and duration distribution.

The functions of silence we observe vary from response preparation to hesitation to asking some queries. It is also observed that sometimes these long silences are used deliberately to get a forced response from another speaker. It can also indicate the indecisiveness of the current speaker.

Even though most of the research from speech communities ignores the silences, our observation shows that by considering the function of long silences, we can better understand the information flow in the conversation. As silences do contribute to explaining the information presented by the speech signals. Silence also has the potential to explain long term behavioral traits and short term states.

This study is our first attempt to analyse, understand and group functions of long silence in dyadic conversations. The observed functions, such as hesitations, are also related to another speech phenomenon – disfluencies. In future work we plan to address the relationship between speech disfluencies and long silences. This analysis will help us to understand the factors and contexts that represent cues of the silence function which is indeed necessary to design computational models for such a simple yet informative event of human conversation.

References

Firoj Alam, Shammur Absar Chowdhury, Morena Danieli, and Giuseppe Riccardi. 2016. How interlocutors coordinate with each other within emotional segments? In *COLING: International Conference on Computational Linguistics*.

Thomas J Bruneau. 1973. Communicative silences: Forms and functions. *Journal of Communication* 23(1):17–46.

Thomas J Bruneau. 2008. How americans use silence and silences to communicate. *China Media Research* 4(2).

Harry Bunt, Jan Alexandersson, Jean Carletta, Jae-Woong Choe, Alex Chengyu Fang, Koiti Hasida, Kiyong Lee, Volha Petukhova, Andrei Popescu-Belis, Laurent Romary, et al. 2010. Towards an ISO standard for dialogue act annotation. In *Seventh conference on International Language Resources and Evaluation (LREC'10)*.

Harry Bunt, Jan Alexandersson, Jae-Woong Choe, Alex Chengyu Fang, Koiti Hasida, Volha Petukhova, Andrei Popescu-Belis, and David R Traum. 2012. ISO 24617-2: A semantically-based standard for dialogue annotation. In *LREC*. pages 430–437.

Joseph N Cappella. 1980. Talk and silence sequences in informal conversations ii. *Human Communication Research* 6(2):130–145.

Shammur A. Chowdhury, Giuseppe Riccardi, and Firoj Alam. 2014. Unsupervised recognition and clustering of speech overlaps in spoken conversations. In *Proc. of Workshop on Speech, Language and Audio in Multimedia*.

Shammur Absar Chowdhury, Evgeny Stepanov, and Giuseppe Riccardi. 2016a. Predicting user satisfaction from turn-taking in spoken conversations. In *Proc. of INTERSPEECH*.

Shammur Absar Chowdhury, Evgeny A. Stepanov, and Giuseppe Riccardi. 2016b. Transfer of corpus-specific dialogue act annotation to iso standard: Is it worth it ? In *Proc. of LREC*.

Michal Ephratt. 2008. The functions of silence. *Journal of Pragmatics* 40(11):1909 – 1938.

D. H. Fisher. 1987. Knowledge acquisition via incremental conceptual clustering. *Machine Learning* 2:139–172.

Ze'ev Frankel, Heidi M Levitt, David M Murray, Leslie S Greenberg, and Lynne Angus. 2006. Assessing silent processes in psychotherapy: An empirically derived categorization system and sampling strategy. *Psychotherapy Research* 16(5):627–638.

John Gale and Beatriz Sanchez. 2005. The meaning and function of silence in psychotherapy with particular reference to a therapeutic community treatment programme. *Psychoanalytic Psychotherapy* 19(3):205–220.

M. A. Gluck and J. E. Corter. 1985. *Information, uncertainty, and the utility of categories*. Proceedings Seventh Annual Conference of the Cognitive Science Society. Lawrence Erlbaum Associates.

Mark Hall, Eibe Frank, Geoffrey Holmes, Bernhard Pfahringer, Peter Reutemann, and Ian H Witten. 2009. The weka data mining software: an update. *ACM SIGKDD Explorations Newsletter* 11(1):10–18.

A. Jaworski. 1993. *The power of silence: social and pragmatic perspectives.* Language and language behaviors. Sage. https://books.google.mu/books?id=0NFoAAAAIAAJ.

J Vernon Jensen. 1973. Communicative functions of silence. *ETC: A Review of General Semantics* pages 249–257.

Masato Kogure. 2007. Nodding and smiling in silence during the loop sequence of backchannels in japanese conversation. *Journal of Pragmatics* 39(7):1275–1289.

Nicholas Ladany, Clara E Hill, Barbara J Thompson, and Karen M O'Brien. 2004. Therapist perspectives on using silence in therapy: A qualitative study. *Counselling and Psychotheraphy Research* 4(1):80–89.

Margaret L McLaughlin and Michael J Cody. 1982. Awkward silences: Behavioral antecedents and consequences of the conversational lapse. *Human communication research* 8(4):299–316.

Joseph Oduro-Frimpong. 2007. Semiotic silence: Its use as a conflictmanagement strategy in intimate relationships. *Semiotica* 2007(167):283–308.

Virginia P Richmond, James C McCroskey, and Steven K Payne. 1991. *Nonverbal behavior in interpersonal relations*. Prentice Hall Englewood Cliffs, NJ.

Elsa Ronningstam. 2006. Cultural function and psychological transformation in psychoanalysis and psychoanalytic psychotherapy. *The International Journal of Psychoanalysis* 87(5):1277–1295.

George R Saunders. 1985. Silence and noise as emotion management styles: An italian case. *Perspectives on silence* pages 165–83.

Deborah Tannen. 1990. Silence as conflict management in fiction and drama: Pinter???s betrayal and a short story, great wits. *Conflict talk: Sociolinguistic investigations of arguments and conversations, ed. AD Grimshaw* pages 260–279.

Don H Zimmermann and Candace West. 1996. Sex roles, interruptions and silences in conversation. *AMSTERDAM STUDIES IN THE THEORY AND HISTORY OF LINGUISTIC SCIENCE SERIES 4* pages 211–236.

Encoding Word Confusion Networks with Recurrent Neural Networks for Dialog State Tracking

Glorianna Jagfeld and **Ngoc Thang Vu**
Institute for Natural Language Processing (IMS)
Universität Stuttgart
Pfaffenwaldring 5B
70569 Stuttgart
{glorianna.jagfeld,thang.vu}@ims.uni-stuttgart.de

Abstract

This paper presents our novel method to encode word confusion networks, which can represent a rich hypothesis space of automatic speech recognition systems, via recurrent neural networks. We demonstrate the utility of our approach for the task of dialog state tracking in spoken dialog systems that relies on automatic speech recognition output. Encoding confusion networks outperforms encoding the best hypothesis of the automatic speech recognition in a neural system for dialog state tracking on the well-known second Dialog State Tracking Challenge dataset.

1 Introduction

Spoken dialog systems (SDSs) allow users to naturally interact with machines through speech and are nowadays an important research direction, especially with the great success of automatic speech recognition (ASR) systems (Mohamed et al., 2012; Xiong et al., 2016). SDSs can be designed for generic purposes, e.g. smalltalk (Weizenbaum, 1966; Vinyals and Le, 2015)) or a specific task such as finding restaurants or booking flights (Bobrow et al., 1977; Wen et al., 2016). Here, we focus on task-oriented dialog systems, which assist the users to reach a certain goal.

Task-oriented dialog systems are often implemented in a modular architecture to break up the complex task of conducting dialogs into more manageable subtasks. Williams et al. (2016) describe the following prototypical set-up of such a modular architecture: First, an ASR system converts the spoken user utterance into text. Then, a spoken language understanding (SLU) module extracts the user's intent and coarse-grained semantic information. Next, a dialog state tracking

(DST) component maintains a distribution over the state of the dialog, updating it in every turn. Given this information, the dialog policy manager decides on the next action of the system. Finally, a natural language generation (NLG) module forms the system reply that is converted into an audio signal via a text-to-speech synthesizer.

Error propagation poses a major problem in modular architectures as later components depend on the output of the previous steps. We show in this paper that DST suffers from ASR errors, which was also noted by Mrksic et al. (2017). One solution is to avoid modularity and instead perform joint reasoning over several subtasks, e.g. many DST systems directly operate on ASR output and do not rely on a separate SLU module (Henderson et al., 2014c; Mrksic et al., 2017; Perez, 2017). End-to-end systems that can be directly trained on dialogs without intermediate annotations have been proposed for open-domain dialog systems (Vinyals and Le, 2015). This is more difficult to realize for task-oriented systems as they often require domain knowledge and external databases. First steps into this direction were taken by Wen et al. (2016) and Zhao and Eskénazi (2016), yet these approaches do not integrate ASR into the joint reasoning process.

We take a first step towards integrating ASR in an end-to-end SDS by passing on a richer hypothesis space to subsequent components. Specifically, we investigate how the richer ASR hypothesis space can improve DST. We focus on these two components because they are at the beginning of the processing pipeline and provide vital information for the subsequent SDS components. Typically, ASR systems output the best hypothesis or an n-best list, which the majority of DST approaches so far uses (Williams, 2014; Henderson et al., 2014c; Mrksic et al., 2017; Zilka and Jurcícek, 2015). However, n-best lists can only

Proceedings of the First Workshop on Speech-Centric Natural Language Processing, pages 10–17
Copenhagen, Denmark, September 7–11, 2017. ©2017 Association for Computational Linguistics

represent a very limited amount of hypotheses. Internally, the ASR system maintains a rich hypothesis space in the form of speech lattices or confusion networks (cnets)[1].

We adapt recently proposed algorithms to encode lattices with recurrent neural networks (RNNs) (Ladhak et al., 2016; Su et al., 2017) to encode cnets via an RNN based on Gated Recurrent Units (GRUs) to perform DST in a neural encoder-classifier system and show that this outperforms encoding only the best ASR hypothesis. We are aware of two DST approaches that incorporate posterior word-probabilities from cnets in addition to features derived from the n-best lists (Williams, 2014; Vodolán et al., 2017), but to the best of our knowledge, we develop the first DST system directly operating on cnets.

2 Proposed Model

Our model depicted in Figure 1 is based on an incremental DST system (Zilka and Jurcícek, 2015). It consists of an embedding layer for the words in the system and user utterances, followed by a fully connected layer composed of Rectified Linear Units (ReLUs) (Glorot et al., 2011), which yields the input to a recurrent layer to encode the system and user outputs in each turn with a softmax classifier on top. $\oplus$ denotes a weighted sum c_j of the system dialog act s_j and the user utterance u_j, where W_s, W_u, and b are learned parameters:

$$c_j = W_s s_j + W_u u_j + b \tag{1}$$

Independent experiments with the 1-best ASR output showed that a weighted sum of the system and user vector outperformed taking only the user vector u_j as in the original model of Zilka and Jurcícek (2015). We chose this architecture over other successful DST approaches that operate on the turn-level of the dialogs (Henderson et al., 2014c; Mrksic et al., 2017) because it processes the system and user utterances word-by-word, which makes it easy to replace the recurrent layer of the original version with the cnet encoder.

Our cnet encoder is inspired from two recently proposed algorithms to encode lattices with an RNN with standard memory (Ladhak et al., 2016) and a GRU-based RNN (Su et al., 2017). In contrast to lattices, every cnet state has only

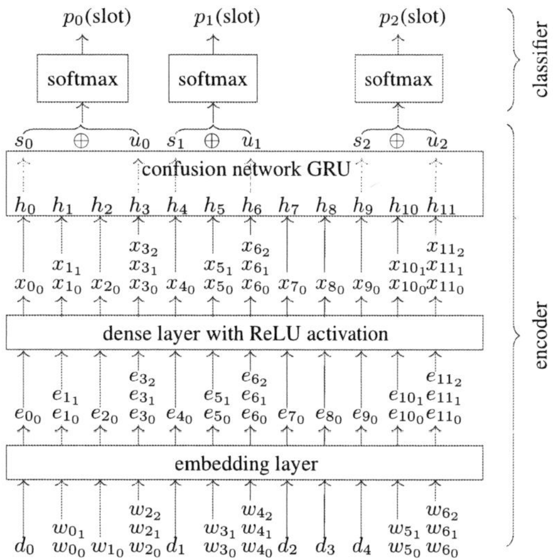

Figure 1: The proposed model with GRU-based cnet encoder for a dialog with three turns. d_t are one-hot word vectors of the system dialog acts; w_{t_i} correspond to the word hypotheses in the timesteps of the cnets of the user utterances; s_j, u_j are the cnet GRU outputs at the end of each system or user utterance.

one predecessor and groups together the alternative word hypotheses of a fixed time interval (timestep). Therefore, our cnet encoder is conceptually simpler and easier to implement than the lattice encoders: The recurrent memory only needs to retain the hidden state of the previous timestep, while in the lattice encoder the hidden states of all previously processed lattice states must be kept in memory throughout the encoding process. Following Su et al. (2017), we use GRUs as they provide an extended memory compared to plain RNNs[2]. The cnet encoder reads in one timestep at a time as depicted in Figure 2. The key idea is to separately process each of the k word hypotheses representations x_{t_i} in a timestep with the standard GRU to obtain k

---

[1]Mangu et al. (2000) show that every speech lattice can be converted to a cnet without losing relevant hypotheses.

[2]Apart from GRUs, long short-term memory (LSTM) cells (Hochreiter and Schmidhuber, 1997) are a more traditional way to extend the recurrent memory. It is still debated which recurrent memory architecture performs best. GRUs are conceptually simpler and have been shown to outperform GRUs for speech signal sequence processing (Chung et al., 2014) and for language modeling with recurrent layers smaller than 200 units (Irie et al., 2016). As our training data is limited, we train models with smaller recurrent layers and therefore use GRUs. Yet, we note that the cnet encoding method can be realized with LSTM cells analogously.

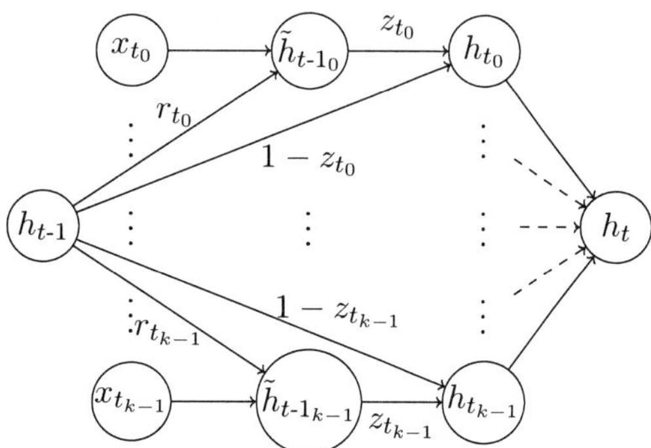

Figure 2: Encoding k alternative hypotheses at timestep t of a cnet.

hidden states h_{t_i} as defined in Equation (2)-(5)[3] where $W_z, U_z, b_z, W_h, U_h, b_h, W_r, U_r$, and b_r are the learned parameters of the GRU update, candidate activation and reset gate. To get the hidden state h_t of the timestep, the hypothesis-specific hidden states h_{t_i} are combined by a pooling function (Equation 6).

$$h_{t_i} = z_{t_i} \cdot h_{t-1} + (1 - z_{t_i}) \cdot \tilde{h}_{t_i} \quad (2)$$
$$z_{t_i} = \sigma(W_z x_{t_i} + U_z h_{t-1} + b_z) \quad (3)$$
$$\tilde{h}_{t_i} = \tanh(W_h x_{t_i} + U_h(r_{t_i} \cdot h_{t-1}) + b_h) \quad (4)$$
$$r_{t_i} = \sigma(W_r x_{t_i} + U_r h_{t-1} + b_r) \quad (5)$$
$$h_t = f_{\text{pool}}(h_{t_0} \ldots h_{t_{k-1}}) \quad (6)$$

We experiment with the two different pooling functions f_{pool} for the k hidden GRU states h_{t_i} of the alternative word hypotheses that were used by Ladhak et al. (2016):

average pooling $\quad f_{average} = \frac{\sum_{i=1}^{k} h_{t_i}}{k}$

weighted pooling $\quad f_{weighted} = \sum_{i=1}^{k} \text{score}_i \cdot h_{t_i}$, where score_i is the confidence score of x_{t_i}.

Instead of the system output in sentence form we use the dialog act representations in the form of ⟨dialog-act, slot, value⟩ triples, e.g. 'inform food Thai', which contain the same information in a more compact way. Following Mrksic et al. (2017), we initialize the word embeddings with 300-dimensional semantically specialized PARAGRAM-SL999 embeddings (Wieting et al., 2015). The hyper-parameters for our model are listed in the appendix.

____
[3]Throughout the paper · denotes an element-wise product.

The cnet GRU subsumes a standard GRU-based RNN if each token in the input is represented as a timestep with a single hypothesis. We adopt this method for the system dialog acts and the baseline model that encode only the best ASR hypothesis.

3   Data

In our experiments, we use the dataset provided for the second Dialog State Tracking Challenge (DSTC2) (Henderson et al., 2014a) that consists of user interactions with an SDS in the restaurant domain. It encompasses 1612, 506, 1117 dialogs for training, development and testing, respectively. Every dialog turn is annotated with its dialog state encompassing the three goals for *area* (7 values), *food* (93 values) and *price range* (5 values) and 8 requestable slots, e.g. phone and address. We train on the manual transcripts and the cnets provided with the dataset and evaluate on the cnets.

Some system dialog acts in the DSTC2 dataset do not correspond to words and thus were not included in the pretrained word embeddings. Therefore, we manually constructed a mapping of dialog acts to words contained in the embeddings, where necessary, e.g. we mapped *expl-conf* to *explicit confirm*.

In order to estimate the potential of improving DST by cnets, we investigated the coverage of words from the manual transcripts for different ASR output types. As shown in Table 1, cnets improve the coverage of words from the transcripts by more than 15 percentage points over the best hypothesis and more than five percentage points over the 10-best hypotheses.

However, the cnets provided with the DSTC2 dataset are quite large. The average cnet consists of 23 timesteps with 5.5 hypotheses each, amounting to about 125 tokens, while the average best hypothesis contains four tokens. Manual inspection of the cnets revealed that they contain a lot of noise such as interjections (*uh, oh, ...*) that never appear in the 10-best lists. The appendix provides an exemplary cnet for illustration. To reduce the processing time and amount of noisy hypotheses, we remove all interjections and additionally experiment with pruning hypotheses with a score below a certain threshold. As shown in Table 1, this does not discard too many correct hypotheses but markedly reduces the size of the cnet to an average of seven timesteps with two hypotheses.

	1-best	10-best	cnet	pruned cnet
all words	69.3	78.6	85.7	83.1
slots/values	69.8	75.6	82.4	80.6

Table 1: Coverage of words from the manual transcripts in the DSTC2 development set of different *batch* ASR output types (%). In the pruned cnet interjections and hypotheses with scores below 0.001 were removed.

4 Results and Discussion

We report the joint goals and requests accuracy (all goals or requests are correct in a turn) according to the DSTC2 featured metric (Henderson et al., 2014a). We train each configuration 10 times with different random seeds and report the average, minimum and maximum accuracy. To study the impact of ASR errors on DST, we trained and evaluated our model on the different user utterance representations provided in the DSTC2 dataset. Our baseline model uses the best hypothesis of the *batch* ASR system, which has a word error rate (WER) of 34% on the DSTC2 test set. Most DST approaches use the hypotheses of the *live* ASR system, which has a lower WER of 29%. We train our baseline on the *batch* ASR outputs as the cnets were also produced by this system. As can be seen from Table 2, the DST accuracy slightly increases for the higher-quality *live* ASR outputs. More importantly, the DST performance drastically increases, when we evaluate on the manual transcripts that reflect the true user utterances nearly perfectly.

test data	goals	requests
train on transcripts + batch ASR (baseline)		
batch ASR	63.6 $^{66.6}_{58.7}$	96.8 $^{97.1}_{96.5}$
train on transcripts + live ASR		
live ASR	63.8 $^{67.0}_{60.2}$	97.5 $^{97.7}_{97.2}$
transcripts	78.3 $^{82.4}_{74.3}$	98.7 $^{99.0}_{98.0}$

Table 2: DSTC2 test set accuracy for 1-best ASR outputs of ten runs with different random seeds in the format average $^{\text{maximum}}_{\text{minimum}}$.

4.1 Results of the Model with Cnet Encoder

Table 3 displays the results for our model evaluated on cnets for increasingly aggressive pruning levels (discarding only interjections, additionally discarding hypotheses with scores below 0.001 and 0.01, respectively). As can be seen, using the full cnet except for interjections does not improve over the baseline. We believe that the share of noisy hypotheses in the DSTC2 cnets is too high for our model to be able to concentrate on the correct hypotheses. However, when pruning low-probability hypotheses both pooling strategies improve over the baseline. Yet, average pooling performs worse for the lower pruning threshold, which shows that the model is still affected by noise among the hypotheses. Conversely, the model can exploit a rich but noisy hypothesis space by weighting the information retained from each hypothesis: Weighted pooling performs better for the lower pruning threshold of 0.001 with which we obtain the highest result overall, improving the joint goals accuracy by 1.6 percentage points compared to the baseline. Therefore, we conclude that is beneficial to use information from all alternatives and not just the highest scoring one but that it is necessary to incorporate the scores of the hypotheses and to prune low-probability hypotheses. Moreover, we see that an ensemble model that averages the predictions of ten cnet models trained with different random seeds also outperforms an ensemble of ten baseline models.

Although it would be interesting to compare the performance of cnets to full lattices, this is not possible with the original DSTC2 data as there were no lattices provided. This could be investigated in further experiments by running a new ASR system on the DSTC2 dataset to obtain both lattices and cnets. However, these results will not be comparable to previous results on this dataset due to the different ASR output.

4.2 Comparison to the State of the Art

The current state of the art on the DSTC2 dataset in terms of joint goals accuracy is an ensemble of neural models based on hand-crafted update rules and RNNs (Vodolán et al., 2017). Besides, this model uses a delexicalization mechanism that replaces mentions of slots or values from the DSTC2 ontology by a placeholder to learn value-independent patterns (Henderson et al., 2014c,b). While this approach is suitable for small domains and languages with a simple morphology such as English, it becomes increasingly difficult to locate

method	goals	requests
1-best baseline	$63.6\,^{66.6}_{58.7}$	$96.8\,^{97.1}_{96.5}$
cnet - no pruning		
weighted pooling	$63.7\,^{65.6}_{61.6}$	$96.7\,^{97.0}_{96.3}$
cnet - score threshold 0.001		
average pooling	$63.7\,^{66.4}_{60.0}$	$96.6\,^{96.8}_{96.0}$
weighted pooling	$\mathbf{65.2}\,^{68.5}_{59.1}$	$97.0\,^{97.4}_{96.6}$
cnet - score threshold 0.01		
average pooling	$64.6\,^{67.9}_{59.7}$	$96.9\,^{97.2}_{96.5}$
weighted pooling	$64.7\,^{68.4}_{62.2}$	$\mathbf{97.1}^{\star}\,^{97.3}_{96.9}$
ensemble models		
baseline	69.7	96.7
cnet	**71.4**	**97.2**
results from related work		
Vodolán et al. (2017)	80.0	-
Williams (2014)	78.4	98.0
Mrksic et al. (2017)	73.4	96.5

Table 3: DSTC2 test set accuracy of ten runs with different random seeds in the format average $^{maximum}_{minimum}$. $\star$ denotes a statistically significant higher result than the baseline ($p < 0.05$, Wilcoxon signed-rank test with Bonferroni correction for ten repeated comparisons). The cnet ensemble corresponds to the best cnet model with pruning threshold 0.001 and weighted pooling.

words or phrases corresponding to slots or values in wider domains or languages with a rich morphology (Mrksic et al., 2017) and we therefore abstained from delexicalization.

The best result for the joint requests was obtained by a ranking model based on hand-crafted features, which relies on separate SLU systems besides ASR (Williams, 2014). SLU is often cast as sequence labeling problem, where each word in the utterance is annotated with its role in respect to the user's intent (Raymond, 2007; Vu et al., 2016), requiring training data with fine-grained word-level annotations in contrast to the turn-level dialog state annotations. Furthermore, a separate SLU component introduces an additional set of parameters to the SDS that has to be learned. Therefore, it has been argued to jointly perform SLU and DST in a single system (Henderson et al., 2014c), which we follow in this work.

As a more comparable reference for our setup, we provide the result of the neural DST system of Mrksic et al. (2017) that like our approach does not use outputs of a separate SLU system nor delexicalized features. Our ensemble models outperform Mrksic et al. (2017) for the joint requests but are a bit worse for the joint goals. We stress that our goal was not to reach for the state of the art but show that DST can benefit from encoding cnets.

5 Conclusion

As we show in this paper, ASR errors pose a major obstacle to accurate DST in SDSs. To reduce the error propagation, we suggest to exploit the rich ASR hypothesis space encoded in cnets that contain more correct hypotheses than conventionally used n-best lists. We develop a novel method to encode cnets via a GRU-based RNN and demonstrate that this leads to improved DST performance compared to encoding the best ASR hypothesis on the DSTC2 dataset.

In future experiments, we would like to explore further ways to leverage the scores of the hypotheses, for example by incorporating them as an independent feature rather than a direct weight in the model.

Acknowledgments

We thank our anonymous reviewers for their helpful feedback. Our work has been supported by the German Research Foundation (DFG) via a research grant to the project A8 within the Collaborative Research Center (SFB) 732 at the University of Stuttgart.

References

Daniel G. Bobrow, Ronald M. Kaplan, Martin Kay, Donald A. Norman, Henry Thompson, and Terry Winograd. 1977. GUS: a Frame-Driven Dialog System. *Artificial Intelligence*, 8.

Junyoung Chung, Caglar Gulcehre, Kyunghyun Cho, and Yoshua Bengio. 2014. Empirical Evaluation of Gated Recurrent Neural Networks on Sequence Modeling. In *Proceedings of the Neural Information Processing Systems (NIPS) Workshop on Deep Learning*.

Xavier Glorot, Antoine Bordes, and Yoshua Bengio. 2011. Deep Sparse Rectifier Neural Networks. In *Proceedings of the Fourteenth International Conference on Artificial Intelligence and Statistics, AIS-TATS*.

Matthew Henderson, Blaise Thomson, and Jason D. Williams. 2014a. The Second Dialog State Tracking Challenge. In *Proceedings of SIGdial*.

Matthew Henderson, Blaise Thomson, and Steve J. Young. 2014b. Robust Dialog State Tracking Using Delexicalised Recurrent Neural Networks and Unsupervised Adaptation. In *Proceedings of IEEE Spoken Language Technology*.

Matthew Henderson, Blaise Thomson, and Steve J. Young. 2014c. Word-based Dialog State Tracking with Recurrent Neural Networks. In *Proceedings of SIGdial*.

Sepp Hochreiter and Jürgen Schmidhuber. 1997. Long Short-Term Memory. *Neural Compututation*, 9(8).

Kazuki Irie, Zoltán Tüske, Tamer Alkhouli, Ralf Schlüter, and Hermann Ney. 2016. LSTM, GRU, Highway and a Bit of Attention: An Empirical Overview for Language Modeling in Speech Recognition. In *Proceedings of Interspeech*.

Faisal Ladhak, Ankur Gandhe, Markus Dreyer, Lambert Matthias, Ariya Rastrow, and Björn Hoffmeister. 2016. LatticeRNN: Recurrent Neural Networks over Lattices. In *Proceedings of Interspeech*.

Lidia Mangu, Eric Brill, and Andreas Stolcke. 2000. Finding consensus in speech recognition: word error minimization and other applications of confusion networks. *Computer Speech & Language*, 14(4).

Abdel-rahman Mohamed, George E. Dahl, and Geoffrey Hinton. 2012. Acoustic Modeling Using Deep Belief Networks. *Transactions on Audio, Speech, and Language Processing*, 20(1).

Nikola Mrksic, Diarmuid Ó Séaghdha, Tsung-Hsien Wen, Blaise Thomson, and Steve J. Young. 2017. Neural Belief Tracker: Data-Driven Dialogue State Tracking. In *Proceedings of ACL*.

Julien Perez. 2017. Dialog state tracking, a machine reading approach using a memory-enhanced neural network. In *Proceedings of EACL*.

Christian Raymond. 2007. Generative and discriminative algorithms for spoken language understanding. In *Proceedings of Interspeech*.

Jinsong Su, Zhixing Tan, Deyi Xiong, Rongrong Ji, Xiaodong Shi, and Yang Liu. 2017. Lattice-Based Recurrent Neural Network Encoders for Neural Machine Translation. In *Proceedings of the Thirty-First AAAI Conference on Artificial Intelligence*.

Oriol Vinyals and Quoc V. Le. 2015. A neural conversational model. In *Proceedings of the International Conference on Machine Learning, Deep Learning Workshop*.

Miroslav Vodolán, Rudolf Kadlec, and Jan Kleindienst. 2017. Hybrid Dialog State Tracker with ASR Features. In *Proceedings of EACL*.

Ngoc Thang Vu, Pankaj Gupta, Heike Adel, and Hinrich Schütze. 2016. Bi-directional Recurrent Neural Network with Ranking Loss for Spoken Language Understanding. In *Proceedings of the IEEE International Conference on Acoustics, Speech and Signal Processing, ICASSP*.

Joseph Weizenbaum. 1966. ELIZA: A Computer Program for the Study of Natural Language Communication Between Man and Machine. *Communications of the ACM*, 9(1).

Tsung-Hsien Wen, Milica Gasic, Nikola Mrksic, Lina Maria Rojas-Barahona, Pei-Hao Su, Stefan Ultes, David Vandyke, and Steve J. Young. 2016. A Network-based End-to-End Trainable Task-oriented Dialogue System. *CoRR*, abs/1604.04562.

John Wieting, Mohit Bansal, Kevin Gimpel, and Karen Livescu. 2015. From Paraphrase Database to Compositional Paraphrase Model and Back. *TACL*, 3.

Jason D. Williams. 2014. Web-style ranking and SLU combination for dialog state tracking. In *Proceedings of SIGdial*.

Jason D. Williams, Antoine Raux, and Matthew Henderson. 2016. The Dialog State Tracking Challenge Series: A Review. *Dialogue and Discourse*, 7(3).

Wayne Xiong, Jasha Droppo, Xuedong Huang, Frank Seide, Mike Seltzer, Andreas Stolcke, Dong Yu, and Geoffrey Zweig. 2016. Achieving human parity in conversational speech recognition. *arXiv preprint arXiv:1610.05256*.

Tiancheng Zhao and Maxine Eskénazi. 2016. Towards End-to-End Learning for Dialog State Tracking and Management using Deep Reinforcement Learning. In *Proceedings of SIGdial*.

Lukás Zilka and Filip Jurcícek. 2015. Incremental LSTM-based Dialog State Tracker. In *Proceedings of the IEEE Workshop on Automatic Speech Recognition and Understanding*.

A. Hyper-Parameters

parameter	value
training epochs	20 (requests), 50 (area, price range), 100 (food)
optimizer	Adam
initial learning rate	0.001
training batch size	10 dialogs
λ of l2 regularization	0.001
dropout rate	0.5
embeddings	pretrained 300-dimensional PARAGRAM-SL999 embeddings
# units GRU	100
# units dense layer	300
size of the system and user vector combination matrix	50
user utterance type training	transcript + cnet
user utterance type testing	cnet

B. Cnet from the DSTC2 Dataset

	start	end	hypotheses with scores
1	0.0328125	0.0492188	!null (-0.0001) uh (-31.83215) ah (-32.41007) i (-34.84077) oh (-40.73034) a (-41.20651)
2	0.0492188	0.065625	!null (-0.0001) i (-36.65728) uh (-48.94583) ah (-52.79816) oh (-55.63619)
3	0.065625	0.0820312	!null (-0.0001) oh (-47.15494)
4	0.0820312	0.0984375	!null (-0.0001) and (-47.59002)
5	0.0984375	0.13125	!null (-0.0001) ah (-33.03135) uh (-39.74279) i'm (-41.90521) i (-42.4907) ok (-42.98212) and (-43.31765) can (-45.37124)
6	0.13125	0.1476562	!null (-0.0001) um (-30.17054) i'm (-32.94894) uh (-35.07708) i (-36.82227) can (-36.89635) and (-36.99255) ah (-43.84253)
7	0.1476562	0.1640625	!null (-0.0001) ah (-41.90521)
8	0.1640625	0.196875	!null (-0.0001) and (-31.41877) ah (-33.03021) i (-34.15576) um (-37.12041) i'm (-37.5037) uh (-40.89799) can (-42.66815)
9	0.196875	0.2296875	!null (-0.0001) ok (-37.41767) i (-43.27491)
10	0.2296875	0.2625	!null (-0.0001) uh (-28.98055) and (-30.48886) i (-30.50464) ah (-31.02539) can (-31.49024) a (-31.74998) um (-39.56715) i'm (-39.6478)
11	0.2625	0.2707031	!null (-0.0001) a (-48.38457)
12	0.2707031	0.2789062	!null (-0.0001) i (-45.51492)
13	0.2789062	0.2953125	!null (-0.0001) uh (-37.77175)
14	0.2953125	0.328125	!null (-0.0001) uh (-22.47343) and (-24.25971) i (-25.13368) can (-31.76437) um (-32.11736) oh (-32.22958) is (-32.77696) ah (-36.18502)
15	0.328125	0.3445312	!null (-0.0001) ah (-25.74752) uh (-29.74647) i (-35.53291) um (-37.89059) oh (-40.87821)
16	0.3445312	0.3609375	!null (-0.0001) uh (-21.97038) oh (-31.83063) ah (-31.96235) i (-42.61901)
17	0.3609375	0.39375	!null (-0.0001) ah (-24.38169) and (-24.39148) ok (-25.08438) i (-29.82585) can (-30.21743) i'm (-33.53017)
18	0.39375	0.525	!null (-0.0001) uh (-23.14362) i (-24.16806) can (-24.21132) um (-24.52006) it (-29.71162) ok (-31.79314) ah (-33.52439) and (-36.14101)
19	0.525	0.590625	!null (-0.0001) ah (-52.30994)
20	0.590625	0.65625	!null (-0.0001) uh (-26.81306)
21	0.65625	0.7875	!null (-0.0001) uh (-17.00693) can (-18.18777) i (-21.7525) and (-22.92453) a (-23.86453) in (-26.00351) ok (-32.25924) ah (-33.28463) it (-37.21361) oh (-45.34864)
22	0.7875	0.8039062	!null (-0.0001) i (-18.35259) and (-18.3801) a (-19.56405) it (-20.65148) is (-20.78921) uh (-22.80336) ok (-23.32806) can (-24.81112) oh (-28.52324)
23	0.8039062	0.8203125	!null (-0.0001) i (-32.22319)
24	0.8203125	0.853125	!null (-0.0001) uh (-9.748239) i (-12.90367) ah (-15.49612) ok (-15.62111) can (-19.96378) and (-23.52033)
25	0.853125	0.8859375	!null (-0.0001) and (-10.25172) uh (-10.51098) i (-14.77064) ok (-17.1938) it (-17.42765) ah (-24.74307)
26	0.8859375	0.91875	!null (-0.0001) ok (-10.7207) and (-14.63778) i (-17.40079)
27	0.91875	0.984375	!null (-0.005078796) and (-5.305283) ok (-9.687913) can (-10.20153) is (-13.44094) uh (-17.34175) where (-23.62194)
28	0.984375	1.05	!null (-0.009671085) ok (-5.591656) could (-5.726142) can (-5.96063) and (-9.760586) it (-17.42122)
29	1.05	1.13	i (-0.003736897) !null (-5.591568) i'd (-14.10718) ok (-20.44036) could (-21.03084)
30	1.13	1.21	!null (-0.003736222) i (-5.59171) could (-15.09615) i'd (-15.67228) thank (-16.10791) it (-16.47987)
31	1.21	1.34	don't (-0.0001) !null (-14.78975) know (-24.44728) gone (-27.63221) i (-28.97229) a (-32.95747) go (-41.58155) da (-47.35928)
32	1.34	1.405	!null (-0.0001) don't (-14.78604) i (-23.63712) a (-24.3221) are (-25.11523) it (-27.08631) uh (-31.06854) of (-32.07071)
33	1.405	1.4375	!null (-0.0001) of (-17.31417) a (-22.29353) ok (-25.30747) i (-30.73294) are (-31.25772)
34	1.4375	1.47	!null (-0.0001) tv (-24.90913) a (-31.64189)
35	1.47	1.5975	care (-0.0001) t (-13.25217) i (-16.79167) to (-19.88062) !null (-22.45499)
36	1.5975	1.725	!null (-0.0001) care (-15.73215)
37	1.725	1.78875	!null (-0.002474642) for (-6.446757) of (-7.396389) food (-8.225521) care (-12.98698) if (-13.04223) and (-16.05245) i (-16.57308) kind (-16.92007) uh (-17.26407) a (-18.45659) or (-18.46813) are (-18.88889) tv (-27.09801)
38	1.78875	1.8525	!null (-0.0001) i (-13.25853) in (-14.35854) of (-17.30617) uh (-20.08914) and (-20.30067) tv (-21.15766) a (-25.55673)
39	1.8525	1.91625	!null (-0.0004876809) the (-7.78335) food (-9.733769) for (-11.98406) i (-12.23129) i'm (-14.38366) of (-18.23437) and (-19.87061)
40	1.91625	1.98	!null (-0.0001) of (-11.92066) the (-11.98383) food (-12.77184) for (-14.38366)

Table 4: Cnet from the DSTC2 development set of the session with id voip-db80a9e6df-20130328_230354. The transcript is *i don't care*, which corresponds the best hypothesis of both ASR systems. Every timestep contains the hypothesis that there is no word (!null).

Analyzing Human and Machine Performance In Resolving Ambiguous Spoken Sentences

Hussein Ghaly[1] and Michael I Mandel[1,2]
[1] City University of New York, Graduate Center, Linguistics Program
[2] City University of New York, Graduate Center, Computer Science Program
{hghaly,mmandel}@gc.cuny.edu

Abstract

Written sentences can be more ambiguous than spoken sentences. We investigate this difference for two different types of ambiguity: prepositional phrase (PP) attachment and sentences where the addition of commas changes the meaning. We recorded a native English speaker saying several of each type of sentence both with and without disambiguating contextual information. These sentences were then presented either as text or audio and either with or without context to subjects who were asked to select the proper interpretation of the sentence. Results suggest that comma-ambiguous sentences are easier to disambiguate than PP-attachment-ambiguous sentences, possibly due to the presence of clear prosodic boundaries, namely silent pauses. Subject performance for sentences with PP-attachment ambiguity without context was 52% for text only while it was 72.4% for audio only, suggesting that audio has more disambiguating information than text. Using an analysis of acoustic features of two PP-attachment sentences, a simple classifier was implemented to resolve the PP-attachment ambiguity being early or late closure with a mean accuracy of 80%.

1   Introduction

There are different kinds of ambiguities in sentence construction, which can be challenging for sentence processing, both in speech and in text. Such ambiguities include structural ambiguities where there can be multiple parse trees for the same sentence. This includes coordination scope ambiguity, such as:

old men and women

which can be parsed as either of the following trees with different meanings:

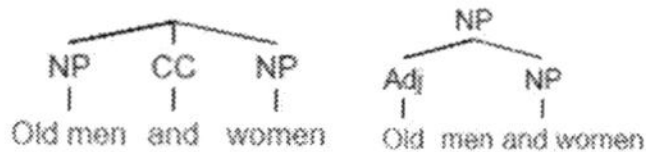

Another example is noun phrase ambiguity, such as:

new project documents

which can be parsed as either of the following trees, again with different meanings:

In speech, prosody has been shown to resolve certain ambiguities when the speaker is able to encode this information (Snedeker and Trueswell, 2003). In order to ensure that the speaker is able to do so, listening tests sometimes engage professional speakers, such as radio announcers, to read the sentence for maximum clarity (Snedeker and Trueswell, 2003).

In particular, Lehiste et al. (1976) found that the duration of words can resolve certain ambiguities reliably, specifically that syntactic boundaries can be perceived by listeners if the duration of the interstress interval at a boundary is increased. Price et al. (1991) found that some, but not all, ambiguities can be resolved on the basis of prosodic differences, where the

Proceedings of the First Workshop on Speech-Centric Natural Language Processing, pages 18–26
Copenhagen, Denmark, September 7–11, 2017. ©2017 Association for Computational Linguistics

disambiguation is related more to the presence of boundaries and to some extent the prominence of certain words. However, when it comes to spontaneous everyday speech, especially by untrained speakers, Tree et al. (2000) found that although listeners can use prosody to resolve ambiguities, contextual information tends to overwhelm it when present. Krajalic and Brennan (2005) point out that results prior to their own study provide mixed evidence for whether speakers spontaneously and reliably produce prosodic cues that resolve syntactic ambiguities.

In text, punctuation can sometimes disambiguate the desired meaning. For example, the sentence:

> 1: A woman without her man is nothing

can mean:

> 1a: A woman, without her man, is nothing.
>
> 1b: A woman, without her, man is nothing.

The insertion of commas changes the meaning of the sentence so that it is not ambiguous when it is read. When each version is spoken, speakers also may encode cues to guide the listeners to the intended meaning. Typical automatic speech recognition output does not include punctuation, leading to transcripts that are ambiguous in this regard, even when the original speech might not be. One solution to this problem is to integrate a separate system for predicting punctuation from speech. For example, this has been done using neural network giving weights to different prosodic cues, where it was possible to predict 54% of the commas (Levy et al., 2012). Other methods include punctuation generation from prosodic cues to improve ASR output (Kim and Woodland, 2001). This is part of recovering the "structural meta-data" from speech, which also includes disfluencies and other sentence boundaries (Liu et al, 2006).

One of the most important ambiguities in both speech and text is prepositional phrase attachment (PP-attachment) ambiguity. A famous examples of this ambiguity is:

> 2: I saw the boy with the telescope.

In this case, no punctuation can help to resolve this structural ambiguity of whether the speaker or the boy had the telescope:

> 2a: I saw the boy [with the telescope]
>
> 2b: I saw [the boy with the telescope]

Snedeker and Trueswell (2003) have shown that this kind of ambiguity can be resolved by prosody in spoken sentences, cuing the different interpretations by the duration of the preposition itself (in this case: "with"), as well as the duration of the following phrase (in this case: "the telescope").

Because prosodic cues, when encoded by the speaker, can help guide the parsing of a structurally ambiguous sentence, we here explicitly compare the abilities of human listeners to disambiguate sentences in both written and spoken form, while starting to build a machine learning system that can perform the same task at least as well.

2 Hypothesis

The main hypothesis in this research is that when there is ambiguity in any sentence and the speaker is aware of the correct reading, they may convey their knowledge of the correct reading using certain prosodic cues. As Snedeker and Trueswell (2003) put it: "informative prosodic cues depend upon speaker's knowledge of the situation: speakers provide prosodic cues when needed; listeners use these prosodic cues when present."

Therefore, for sentences with comma ambiguity, given the correct punctuation, we can expect speakers to encode prosodic cues in their speech accordingly, and we can expect listeners to process these cues in their understanding of the sentence. For sentences with PP-attachment ambiguity, given a preceding disambiguating sentence, speakers may encode prosodic cues to indicate the intended meaning.

3 Goal

The ultimate goal of this research is to use prosody to improve parsing of ambiguous spoken sentences, allowing extracting information from speech that is not available from text only. This involves analyzing human disambiguation behavior for scripted sentences while building a machine learning system to automatically perform this disambiguation.

4 Data

Two types of sentences were investigated: sentences with comma ambiguities and sentences with PP-attachment ambiguity. We constructed 12 pairs of sentences with comma ambiguity and 14 pairs of sentences with PP-attachment ambiguity, as shown in the appendix.

4.1 Comma-ambiguous sentences

An example of a pair of comma-ambiguous sentences is:

> 3a: John, said Mary, was the nicest person at the party.
> 3b: John said Mary was the nicest person at the party.

These sentences are presented individually to the subject along with the question:

> Who was said to be the nicest person at the party?
> A: John
> B: Mary

The correct answer for sentence 3a is A and for 3b is B.

4.2 PP-attachment sentences

An example of a pair of PP-attachment ambiguous sentences is:

> 4a: *One of the boys got a telescope.* I saw the boy with the telescope.
> 4b:- *I have a new telescope.* I saw the boy with the telescope.

The initial italic sentence guides the speaker to the intended reading and in different experimental conditions were included or not included in the presentations to listening or reading subjects to measure their informativeness. The correct parse of sentence 4a exhibits "late closure":

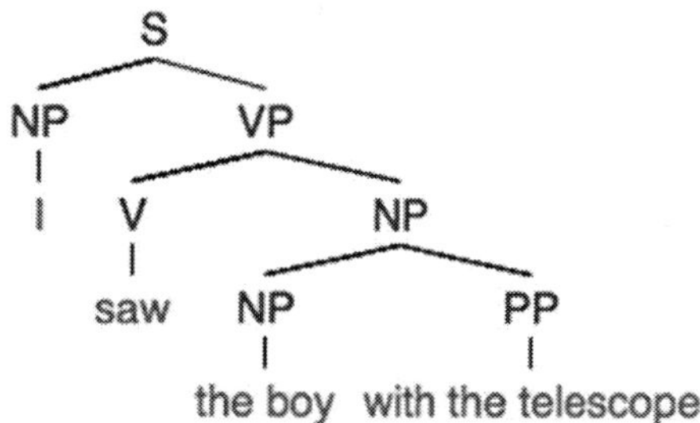

The correct parse of sentence 4b exhibits early closure:

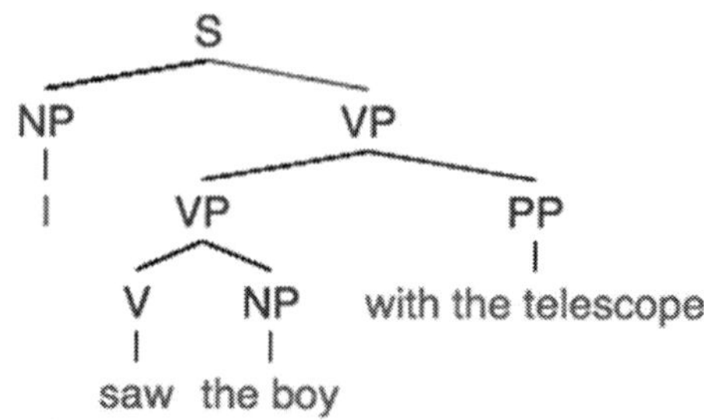

These sentences are presented individually to the subject along with the question:

> Who has the telescope?
> A: The boy
> B: The speaker

The correct answer for sentence 4a is A and for 4b is B.

5 Method

5.1 Speech Data Collection

A native speaker of English recorded the complete list of 26 unique sentences, through a custom web interface implemented using Javascript and Python CGI. Each sentence was repeated five times and the 130 sentence instances were randomized before presentation to the speaker. PP-attachment ambiguous sentences were presented to the speaker with preceding context sentences, as in 4a and 4b. For the below experiments, all of the sentences with their text and audio are presented to the listeners.

5.2 Listener interface

Listener responses were also collected via another custom web interface. An example interface page is shown below:

5.3   Listener tasks

Sentences were presented to subjects either in written form or in recorded audio form. PP-attachment sentences were presented either with or without the preceding context sentence both for written and audio modalities. The tasks were presented in the following order, each one including a randomized ordering of all of the sentences:

1- Comma-ambiguity - Text

2- Comma-ambiguity - Audio

3- PP-attachment ambiguity with context - Text

4- PP-attachment ambiguity with context - Audio

5- PP-attachment ambiguity without context - Text

6- PP-attachment ambiguity without context - Audio

This order aims to familiarize the listeners gradually with the task by showing the text sentences first, which also serves as benchmark to detect any biases or confusion regarding the sentence itself. It then proceeds to the corresponding audio. The sequence follows a gradual increase of difficulty, saving for last the most difficult task: PP-attachment disambiguation without context in text and then audio.

6 Results

Four listeners participated in the study. Two of them were native English speakers. Their accuracy in identifying which of two possible meanings the speaker was cued is shown in the following table.

Ambiguity	Modality	Accuracy
Comma	Text	99.3%
Comma	Audio	94.7%
PP-attachment with context	Text	93.1%
PP-attachment with context	Audio	97.1%
PP-attachment without context	Text	52.0%
PP-attachment without context	Audio	74.4%

These results show that humans are quite good at interpreting comma-ambiguous sentences in both text and speech modalities. For PP-attachment, they also perform well for both modalities when the preceding context sentence is provided. Without the context sentence, they perform at chance for text, but much better than chance for speech, showing that there is, indeed, additional information present in the speech. Because performance is at ceiling for comma-ambiguity, we focus our subsequent analysis on the PP-attachment sentences.

The following table shows results for each of the PP-attachments sentences presented as speech without context. All productions of each version of each sentence are grouped together.

Sentence	Accuracy	N
1: I saw the boy with the telescope.	68.9%	29
2: I saw the man with the new glasses.	78.6%	28
3: San Jose cops kill a man with a knife.	89.3%	28
4: They discussed the mistakes in the second meeting.	70.9%	31
5: The lawyer contested the proceedings in the third hearing.	63.3%	31
6: He used the big wrench in the car.	82.1%	28
7: I waited for the man in the red car.	68.9%	29

In order to investigate the role of prosodic features in this disambiguation, we performed a preliminary semi-automatic analysis of the recordings of two of these sentences. A number of acoustic features were measured manually in Praat for all of the productions of both versions of two of the PP-attachment sentences, numbers

4 and 5. Following Levy et al (2012), we measured the following features:

- duration of the preposition utterance (in milliseconds)
- duration of the silent pause (if any) preceding the preposition (in milliseconds)
- duration of the noun phrase following the preposition (in milliseconds)
- Intensity of the preposition (in decibels)

By manually extracting features, we achieve an upper bound on the performance of an automatic feature extraction procedure.

In order to examine the minimum level of acoustic cues encoded by the speaker to see if it is still possible to extract meaningful patterns that can be used for automatic systems, we examine the sentences that listeners were unable to classify correctly.

As shown in the preceding table, one of the worst performing sentence for the PP-attachment disambiguation task from audio without context was:

4: They discussed the mistakes in the second meeting.

This sentence was correctly identified only 70.9% of the time, mostly being mistaken for early closure when in fact it was late closure, as shown in the detailed results in Appendix 2. This was not the case for this particular sentence for the audio with context or text with context.

The other sentence with most inaccurate disambiguation results (63.3% accuracy, evenly distributed between classes) was:

5: The lawyer contested the proceedings in the third hearing.

The following table shows the acoustic feature values averaged over the 20 productions of sentences 4 and 5. Note that both sentences use the same preposition and have the same number of words in the noun phrase following it.

	Late	Early
Preposition Duration (ms)	147	143
Preceding silent pauses (ms)	0	48
Intensity (dB)	57.84	56.37

Following NP duration (ms)	579	639.5

Using these data, we implemented a simple decision tree classifier to predict the closure type. Using 5-fold cross validation, the mean accuracy was 80%. The major node in the decision tree was the existence of a silent pause of smaller duration than 20 ms.

7 Conclusion

Although there has been much research in psychology regarding the perception of ambiguous sentences, more still needs to be done to model such sentences to facilitate integration with ASR systems, as well as question answering systems and natural language understanding.

The current research attempts to start developing this model. This is first done by quantifying human perception of certain ambiguous sentences, and analyzing these sentences acoustically to extract prosodic cues that can be used as features in a machine learning model for classifying sentences and deciding on their intended structure accordingly.

We found in our experiments that humans were able to disambiguate sentences with comma ambiguity at ceiling performance levels both as text and speech. For sentences with PP-attachment without context, human performance on text was close to chance at 52%, while for audio it was 74.4%, suggesting a richness of acoustic cues that can guide this ambiguation.

The machine learning model developed revealed the importance of the existence of a silent pause before the prepositional phrase as a major factor in determining the type of attachment. This, however, shouldn't preclude the possible effects of other features and combinations thereof. For example, the average duration of the following NP was shorter for early closure than for late closure. These classifier results are preliminary given the very small size of the dataset.

Going forward, more speech samples need to be generated from multiple speakers. More listeners are needed to provide more certainty about the human ability to disambiguate. And these data can be analyzed in many more ways, both in terms of human perception and automatic classification.

As for extracting the acoustic features, a very important step is to use a forced alignment tool to measure the durations and starting and ending times for each word with greater accuracy and in a way that can be automated for a large number of speech files.

With more of both the human disambiguation data and acoustic data of the corresponding sentences, it will be possible to allow better parsing of ambiguous sentences from speech and the output of ASR systems.

8   Acknowledgements

We would like to thank Professors Janet Dean Fodor and Jason Bishop for their continuous support.

9   References

Kim, Ji-Hwan, and Philip C. Woodland. "The use of prosody in a combined system for punctuation generation and speech recognition." INTERSPEECH. 2001.

Kraljic, Tanya, and Susan E. Brennan. "Prosodic disambiguation of syntactic structure: For the speaker or for the addressee?." Cognitive psychology 50.2 (2005): 194-231.

Lehiste, Ilse, Joseph P. Olive, and Lynn A. Streeter. "Role of duration in disambiguating syntactically ambiguous sentences." The Journal of the Acoustical Society of America 60.5 (1976): 1199-1202.

Levy, Tal, Vered Silber-Varod, and Ami Moyal. "The effect of pitch, intensity and pause duration in punctuation detection." Electrical & Electronics Engineers in Israel (IEEEI), 2012 IEEE 27th Convention of. IEEE, 2012.

Liu, Yang, et al. "Enriching speech recognition with automatic detection of sentence boundaries and disfluencies." IEEE Transactions on audio, speech, and language processing 14.5 (2006): 1526-1540.

Price, Patti J., et al. "The use of prosody in syntactic disambiguation." the Journal of the Acoustical Society of America 90.6 (1991): 2956-2970.

Snedeker, Jesse, and John Trueswell. "Using prosody to avoid ambiguity: Effects of speaker awareness and referential context." Journal of Memory and language 48.1 (2003): 103-130.

Tree, Jean E. Fox, and Paul JA Meijer. "Untrained speakers' use of prosody in syntactic disambiguation and listeners' interpretations." Psychological Research 63.1 (2000): 1-13.

Appendix 1 - List of Sentences

Sentence ID	Sentance	Type
1a	I have a new telescope. I saw the boy with the telescope.	late closure
1b	One of the boys got a telescope. I saw the boy with the telescope.	early closure
2a	She gave me new glasses. I saw the man with the new glasses.	late closure
2b	One of the men bought new glasses. I saw the man with the new glasses.	early closure
3a	Protests against knife-wielding cops. San Jose cops kill a man with a knife.	late closure
3b	Another man shot by the cops. San Jose cops kill a man with a knife.	early closure
4a	The project was full of mistakes. They discussed the mistakes in the second meeting.	late closure
4b	The second meeting was full of mistakes. They discussed the mistakes in the second meeting.	early closure
5a	The third hearing was full of problems. The lawyer contested the proceedings in the third hearing.	early closure
5b	The lawyer keeps complaining about the proceedings. The lawyer contested the proceedings in the third hearing.	late closure
6a	He bought a big wrench. He used the big wrench in the car.	late closure
6b	He was looking for any tool. He used the big wrench in the car.	early closure
7a	I rented a red car. I waited for the man in the red car.	late closure
7b	She told me he has a red car. I waited for the man in the red car.	early closure
8a	John, said Mary, was the nicest person at the party.	with commas
8b	John said Mary was the nicest person at the party.	without commas
9a	Adam, said Anna, was the smartest person in class.	with commas
9b	Adam said Anna was the smartest person in class.	without commas
10a	The teacher, said the student, didn't understand the question.	with commas
10b	The teacher said the student didn't understand the question.	without commas
11a	The neighbors, said my father, parked the car in the wrong spot.	with commas
11b	The neighbors said my father parked the car in the wrong spot.	without commas
12a	The new manager, said my colleague, is very lazy.	with commas
12b	The new manager said my colleague is very lazy.	without commas
13a	The author, said the journalist, didn't address the main problem.	with commas
13b	The author said the journalist didn't address the main problem.	without commas

Appendix 2- Detailed results by sentence for PP-attachment ambiguity

Ambiguous?	Modality	Sentence ID	Mistake	Total
ambiguous	audio	1a	5	14
ambiguous	txt	1a	2	8
context	audio	1a	0	14
context	txt	1a	1	10
ambiguous	audio	1b	4	15
ambiguous	txt	1b	5	9
context	audio	1b	0	15
context	txt	1b	1	12
ambiguous	audio	2a	5	15
ambiguous	txt	2a	7	9
context	audio	2a	1	16
context	txt	2a	1	13
ambiguous	audio	2b	1	13
ambiguous	txt	2b	2	8
context	audio	2b	0	13
context	txt	2b	0	9
ambiguous	audio	3a	1	14
ambiguous	txt	3a	5	6
context	audio	3a	0	14
context	txt	3a	0	12
ambiguous	audio	3b	2	14
ambiguous	txt	3b	3	11
context	audio	3b	0	15
context	txt	3b	2	11
ambiguous	audio	4a	1	15
ambiguous	txt	4a	6	10
context	audio	4a	1	15
context	txt	4a	1	13
ambiguous	audio	4b	8	16
ambiguous	txt	4b	5	9
context	audio	4b	1	16
context	txt	4b	1	12
ambiguous	audio	5a	5	14
ambiguous	txt	5a	4	6
context	audio	5a	0	14
context	txt	5a	0	10
ambiguous	audio	5b	6	16
ambiguous	txt	5b	4	12
context	audio	5b	3	16
context	txt	5b	3	12
ambiguous	audio	6a	3	13
ambiguous	txt	6a	7	8
context	audio	6a	0	13
context	txt	6a	0	10
ambiguous	audio	6b	2	15
ambiguous	txt	6b	2	9
context	audio	6b	0	16
context	txt	6b	1	12
ambiguous	audio	7a	6	15
ambiguous	txt	7a	4	8
context	audio	7a	0	15
context	txt	7a	0	11
ambiguous	audio	7b	3	14
ambiguous	txt	7b	3	10
context	audio	7b	0	15
context	txt	7b	0	12

Appendix 3: Detailed feature values

Acoustic feature for productions of sentence 4:

File #	duration of preposition (ms)	preceding silence (ms)	following NP duration (ms)	Preposition Intensity (dB)	Closure Type
1	160	0	690	56.6	early
3	175	0	660	59.0	late
26	120	0	470	56.2	late
51	140	80	620	55.6	early
67	145	0	600	58.7	late
76	140	90	635	57.8	early
78	135	0	510	61.1	late
82	150	110	600	57.9	early
109	130	0	620	61.0	late
121	140	60	580	58.8	early

Acoustic features for productions of sentence 5:

File #	duration of preposition (ms)	preceding silence (ms)	following NP duration (ms)	Preposition Intensity (dB)	Closure Type
18	140	20	660	54.6	early
21	170	0	580	54.8	late
44	160	0	630	53.8	late
46	140	0	680	50.8	early
52	160	0	550	58.0	late
75	140	80	680	56.1	early
81	160	0	640	58.3	early
83	150	0	600	59.6	late
113	125	0	570	56.2	late
115	120	40	610	57.2	early

Parsing transcripts of speech

Andrew Caines
ALTA Institute
University of Cambridge
apc38@cam.ac.uk

Michael McCarthy
School of English
University of Nottingham
mactoft@cantab.net

Paula Buttery
Computer Laboratory
University of Cambridge
pjb48@cam.ac.uk

Abstract

We present an analysis of parser performance on speech data, comparing word
type and token frequency distributions
with written data, and evaluating parse
accuracy by length of input string. We
find that parser performance tends to de-
teriorate with increasing length of string,
more so for spoken than for written texts.
We train an alternative parsing model with
added speech data and demonstrate improvements in accuracy on speech-units,
with no deterioration in performance on
written text.

1 Introduction

Relatively little attention has been paid to parsing spoken language compared to parsing written
language. The majority of parsers are built using
newswire training data and *The Wall Street Journal* section 21 of the Penn Treebank is a ubiquitous
test set. However, the parsing of speech is of no
little importance, since it's the primary mode of
communication worldwide, and human computer
interaction through the spoken modality is increasingly common.

In this paper we first describe the morpho-
syntactic characteristics of spoken language and
point out some key distributional differences with
written language, and the implications for parsing. We then investigate how well a commonly-
used open source parser performs on a corpus of
spoken language and corpora of written language,
showing that performance deteriorates sooner for
speech as the length of input string increases. We
demonstrate that a new parsing model trained on
both written and spoken data brings improved performance, making this model freely available[1]. Fi-

nally we consider a modification to deal with long
input strings in spoken language, a preprocessing
step which we plan to implement in future work.

2 Spoken language

As has been well described, speech is very different in nature to written language (Brazil, 1995;
Biber et al., 1999; Leech, 2000; Carter and Mc-
Carthy, 2017). Putting aside the mode of transmis-
sion for now – the phonetics and prosody of pro-
ducing speech versus the graphemics and orthog-
raphy of writing systems – we focus on morphology, syntax and vocabulary: that is, the components of speech we can straightforwardly analyse
in transcriptions. We also put aside pragmatics and
discourse analysis therefore, even though there is
much that is distinctive in speech, including intonation and co-speech gestures to convey meaning,
and turn-taking, overlap and co-construction in di-
alogic interaction.

A fundamental morpho-syntactic characteristic
of speech is the lack of the sentence unit used by
convention in writing, delimited by a capital let-
ter and full stop (period). Indeed it has been said
that, "such a unit does not realistically exist in conversation" (Biber et al., 1999). Instead in spoken
language we refer to 'speech-units' (SUs)– token
sequences which are usually coherent units from
the point of view of syntax, semantics, prosody,
or some combination of the three (Strassel, 2003).
Thus we are able to model SU boundaries prob-
abilistically, and find that, in dialogue at least,
they often coincide with turn-taking boundaries
(Shriberg et al., 2000; Lee and Glass, 2012; Moore
et al., 2016).

Other well-known characteristics of speech are
disfluencies such as hesitations, repetitions and
false starts (1)-(3).

(1) um he's a closet yuppie is what he is (Leech,

---

[1]https://goo.gl/iQMu9w

27

Proceedings of the First Workshop on Speech-Centric Natural Language Processing, pages 27–36
Copenhagen, Denmark, September 7–11, 2017. ©2017 Association for Computational Linguistics

2000).

(2) I played, I played against um (Leech, 2000).

(3) You're happy to – welcome to include it (Levelt, 1989).

Disfluencies are pervasive in speech: of an annotated 767k token subset of the Switchboard Corpus of telephone conversations (SWB), 17% are disfluent tokens of some kind (Meteer et al., 1995). Furthermore they are known to cause problems in natural language processing, as they must be incorporated in the parse tree or somehow removed (Nasr et al., 2014). Indeed an 'edit' transition has been proposed specifically to deal with automatically identified disfluencies, by removing them from the parse tree constructed up to that point along with any associated grammatical relations (Honnibal and Johnson, 2014; Moore et al., 2015). We compared the SWB portion of Penn Treebank 3 (Marcus et al., 1999) with the three English corpora contained in Universal Dependencies 2.0 (Nivre et al., 2017) as a representation of the written language. These are namely:

- The 'Universal Dependencies English Web Treebank' (EWT), the English Web Treebank in dependency format (Bies et al., 2012; Silveira et al., 2014);

- 'English LinES' (LinES), the English section of a parallel corpus of English novels and Swedish translations (Ahrenberg, 2015);

- The 'Treebank of Learner English' (TLE), a manually annotated subset of the Cambridge Learner Corpus First Certificate in English dataset (Yannakoudakis et al., 2011; Berzak et al., 2016).

We found several differences between our spoken and written datasets in terms of morphological, syntactic and lexical features. Firstly, the most frequent tokens in writing (ignoring punctuation marks) are, unsurprisingly, function words – determiners, prepositions, conjunctions, pronouns, auxiliary and copula verbs, and the like (Table 1). These are normally considered 'stopwords' in large-scale linguistic analyses, but even if they are semantically uninteresting, their ranking is indicative of differences between speech and writing.

Speech	Freq.	Rank	Writing	Freq.
I	46,382	1	the	41,423
and	33,080	2	to	26,459
the	29,870	3	and	22,977
you	27,142	4	I	20,048
that	27,038	5	a	18,289
it	26,600	6	of	18,112
to	22,666	7	in	14,490
a	22,513	8	is	10,020
uh	20,695	9	you	10,002
's	20,494	10	that	9952
of	17,112	11	for	8578
yeah	14,805	12	it	8238
know	14,723	13	was	8195
they	13,147	14	have	6604
in	12,548	15	on	5821
do	12,507	16	with	5621
n't	11,100	17	be	5514
we	10,308	18	are	4815
have	9970	19	not	4716
uh-huh	9325	20	my	4478

Table 1: The most frequently occurring tokens in selected corpora of English speech (the Switchboard Corpus in Penn Treebank 3) and writing (EWT, LinES, TLE), normalised to counts per million.

In SWB the most frequent token is *I* followed by *and*, then *the* albeit much less frequently than in writing, then *you, that, it* at much higher relative frequencies (per million tokens) than in writing. This ranking reflects the way that (telephone) conversations revolve around the first and second person (*I* and *you*), and the way that speech makes use of coordination and hence the conjunction *and* much more than writing.

Furthermore clitics indicative of possession, copula or auxiliary *be*, or negation (*'s, n't*) and discourse markers *uh, yeah, uh-huh* are all in the twenty-five most frequent terms in SWB. The single content word in these top-ranked tokens (assuming *have* occurs mainly as an auxiliary) is *know*, 13th most frequent in SWB, but as will become clear in Table 3, it's hugely boosted by its use in the fixed phrase, *you know*.

Finally we note that the normalised frequencies for these most frequent tokens are higher in speech than in writing, suggesting that there is greater distributional mass in fewer token types in SWB, a suggestion borne out by sampling 394,611 tokens (the sum total of the three written corpora) from SWB 100 times and finding that not once does the vocabulary size exceed even half that of the written corpora (Table 2).

With the most frequent bigrams we note further differences between speech and writing (Ta-

Medium	Tokens	Types
speech	394,611*	11,326**
writing	394,611	27,126

Table 2: Vocabulary sizes in selected corpora of English speech and writing (* sampled from 766,560 tokens in SWB corpus; ** mean of 100 samples, st.dev=45.5).

ble 3). The most frequent bigrams in writing tend to be combinations of preposition and determiner, or pronoun and auxiliary verb. In speech on the other hand, the very frequent bigrams include the discourse markers *you know, I mean*, and *kind of*, pronoun plus auxiliary or copula *it's, that's, I'm, they're*, and *I've*, and disfluent repetition *I I*, and hesitation *and uh*. Again frequency counts are lower for the written corpus, symptomatic of a smaller set of bigrams in speech. There are 163,690 unique bigrams in the written data, and a mean of 89,787 (st.dev=151) unique bigrams in SWB from 100 samples.

Speech	Freq.	Rank	Writing	Freq.
you know	11,165	1	of the	4313
it's	8531	2	in the	3702
that's	6708	3	to the	2352
don't	5680	4	I have	1655
I do	4390	5	on the	1607
I think	4142	6	I am	1500
and I	3790	7	for the	1475
I'm	3716	8	I would	1427
I I	3000	9	and the	1389
in the	2972	10	and I	1361
and uh	2780	11	to be	1318
a lot	2714	12	I was	1140
of the	2655	13	don't	1125
it was	2616	14	will be	1092
I mean	2518	15	it was	1057
kind of	2448	16	at the	1044
they're	2349	17	in a	1041
I've	2165	18	like to	1036
going to	2135	19	is a	1021
lot of	2053	20	it is	998

Table 3: The most frequently occurring bigrams in selected corpora of English speech (the Switchboard Corpus in Penn Treebank 3) and writing (EWT, LinES, TLE), normalised to counts per million.

In Table 4 we present a short list of the most frequent dependency types, represented as part-of-speech tag pairs $\text{TAG}_1\_\text{TAG}_2$, where TAG_1 is the head and TAG_2 is the dependent. In speech we see that several of the most frequent dependency pairs involve a verb or root as the head, whereas the most frequent pairs in writing involve a noun.

We are certain that in future work there are fur-

Speech	Freq.	Rank	Writing	Freq.
VBP_PRP	51,845	1	NN_DT	48,846
NN_DT	47,469	2	NN_IN	36,274
ROOT_UH	39,067	3	NN_NN	27,490
IN_NN	26,868	4	NN_JJ	21,566
VB_PRP	24,321	5	VB_NN	19,584
ROOT_VBP	24,156	6	VB_PRP	16,320

Table 4: The most frequently occurring part-of-speech tag dependency pairs in selected corpora of English speech (the Switchboard Corpus in Penn Treebank 3) and writing (EWT, LinES, TLE), normalised to counts per million. The first tag in the pair is the head of the relation; the second is the dependent (Penn Treebank tagset).

ther insights to be gleaned from comparisons of speech and writing at higher-order *n*-grams and in terms of dependency relations between tokens. These may in turn have implications for parsing algorithms, or at least may suggest some solutions for more accurate parsing of speech. Other genres and styles of speech and writing would also be worthy of study – especially more recently collected recordings of speech.

3 Parsing experiments

We used the Stanford CoreNLP toolkit (Manning et al., 2014) to tokenize, tag and parse input strings from a range of corpora. This includes the 766k token section of the Switchboard Corpus of telephone conversations (SWB) distributed as part of Penn Treebank 3 (Godfrey et al., 1992; Marcus et al., 1999), and English treebanks from the Universal Dependencies release 2 (Nivre et al., 2017). All treebanks are in CoNLL format[2] and we measure performance through unlabelled attachment scores (UAS) which indicate the proportion of tokens with correctly identified heads in the output of the parser, compared with gold-standard annotations (Kübler et al., 2009).

In Table 5 we report UAS scores overall for each corpus, along with corpus sizes in terms of tokens and sentence or speech units. It is apparent that (a) parser performance for speech units is much poorer than for written units, and that (b) performance across written corpora is broadly similar, though TLE (surprisingly) has the highest UAS score – possibly reflective of a tendency for language learners to write in syntactically more con-

---

[2] We thank Matthew Honnibal for sharing the SWB treebank converted to CoNLL-X format, arising from his TACL paper with Mark Johnson (Honnibal and Johnson, 2014).

servative ways [an issue we won't explore further here].

Corpus	Medium	Units	Tokens	UAS
SWB	speech	102,900	766,560	.540
EWT	writing	14,545	218,159	.744
LinES	writing	3650	64,188	.758
TLE	writing	5124	96,180	.845

Table 5: Corpus sizes and overall unlabelled attachment scores using Stanford Core NLP; SWB=Switchboard, EWT=English Web Treebank, LinES=English section LinES, TLE=Treebank of Learner English

Closer inspection of UAS scores by speech unit in SWB shows that parser performance is not uniformly worse than it is for written language. If we sort the input units into bins by unit length, we see that the parser is as accurate for shorter units of transcribed speech as it is for written units of similar lengths (Table 6)[3]. Indeed for speech units of 1-10 tokens in SWB, mean UAS is similar to that for sentence units of 1-10 tokens in EWT. However, the main difference in UAS scores over increasingly long inputs is the rate of deterioration in parser performance: for speech units the drop-off in UAS scores is much steeper.

Even with strings up to 40 tokens in length, mean UAS remains within 10 points of that for the 1-10 token bin in the three written corpora. But for SWB, mean UAS by that point is less than 50%. In fact in the 11-20 token bin we already see a steep drop-off in parser performance compared to the shortest class of speech unit.

It is only above 50 tokens that EWT and LinES UAS means fall by more than 10 percentage points compared to the 1-10 token score; for TLE this is true above 60 tokens. By this stage we are dealing with small proportions of the written corpora: 96.9% of the units in EWT and 98.1% in LinES are of length 50 tokens or fewer, whilst 99.8% of units in TLE are 60 tokens or shorter (Figure 1).

For SWB the problem is more acute, with 25.5% of units at least 11 tokens long and scoring mean UAS 50% or less. Figure 2 illustrates the disparity with boxplots showing UAS medians (thick line), first and third quartiles ('hinges' at bottom and top of box), ± 1.5 inter-quartile range from the hinge (whiskers), and outliers beyond this range. It is apparent that parser performance

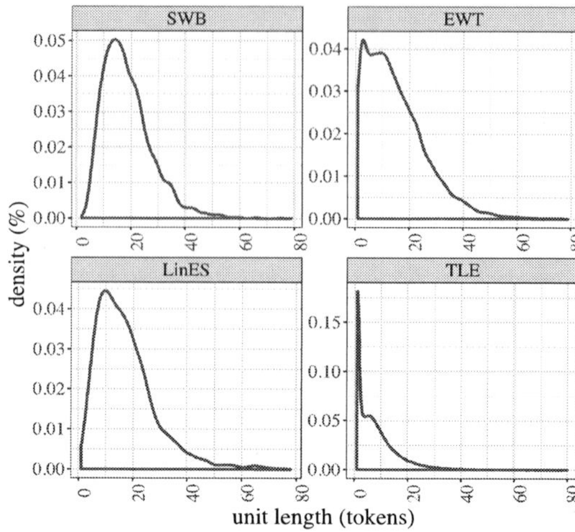

Figure 1: Density plot of unit lengths in four English corpora; SWB=Switchboard, EWT=English Web Treebank, LinES=English section LinES, TLE=Treebank of Learner English.

deteriorates as the unit length increases, for all corpora, but especially so for the speech corpus SWB.

What can be done to address this problem? One approach is to train a new parsing model on more appropriate training data, since general-purpose open-source parsers are usually trained on sections of *The Wall Street Journal* (WSJ) in Treebank 3 (Marcus et al., 1999). Training NLP tools with data appropriate to the medium, genre, or domain, is generally thought to be sensible and helpful to the task (Caines and Buttery, 2014; Plank, 2016). We do not claim this to be a groundbreaking proposal therefore, but instead present the results of such a step here for three reasons:

(i) To demonstrate how much improvement can be gained with a domain-appropriate parsing model;

(ii) To make the speech parsing model publicly available for other researchers;

(iii) To call for greater availability of speech transcript treebanks.

With regard to point (iii), to the best of our knowledge, the Switchboard portion of the Penn Treebank (PTB) is the only substantial, readily-available[4] treebank for spoken English. We welcome feedback to the contrary, and efforts to pro-

---

[3]Units longer than 80 tokens are omitted from the analysis as there are too few for meaningful comparison.

[4]Subject to licence available from the Linguistic Data Consortium.

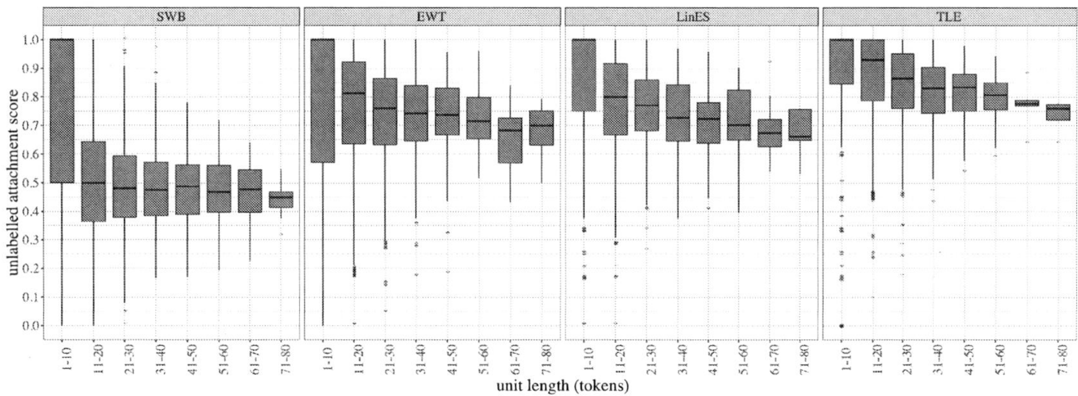

Figure 2: Unlabelled attachment scores by unit length in four English corpora.

Corpus	Unit length (tokens)							
	1-10	11-20	21-30	31-40	41-50	51-60	61-70	71-80
SWB	.753 (76232)	.506 (19281)	.489 (4885)	.480 (1344)	.480 (366)	.473 (126)	.460 (37)	.447 (12)
EWT	.759 (6011)	.762 (4680)	.738 (2453)	.731 (944)	.736 (312)	.718 (96)	.655 (30)	.684 (12)
LinES	.826 (1086)	.770 (1433)	.761 (720)	.731 (251)	.710 (89)	.713 (37)	.674 (24)	.671 (5)
TLE	.866 (887)	.866 (2410)	.838 (1302)	.817 (380)	.816 (101)	.799 (34)	.770 (5)	.733 (4)

Table 6: Unlabelled attachment scores by unit length in four English corpora (number of units in parentheses).

duce new treebanks. Furthermore, if this is the situation for as well-resourced a language as English, we assume that the need for treebanks of speech corpora is even greater for other languages.

In point (ii) we don't imagine we're making a definitive statement on the best model for parsing speech – rather we think of it as a baseline against which future models can be compared. We welcome contributions in this respect.

As for point (i), we trained two new parsing models using the Stanford Parser (Klein and Manning, 2003). These were based on the WSJ sections of PTB as is standard, with added training data from SWB setting the maximum unit length first at 40 tokens – which appears to be the standard length for the models distributed with the parser – and secondly at an increased maximum of 80 tokens. Both were probabilistic context-free grammars. We refer to them as PCFG_WSJ_SWB_40 and PCFG_WSJ_SWB_80.

In Table 7 we show overall UAS scores for our four target English corpora, for three parsing models: the standard model distributed with CoreNLP, and our two new models, PCFG_WSJ_SWB_40 and PCFG_WSJ_SWB_80. It is apparent that the new models bring a large performance gain in parsing speech, as expected, plus a small performance gain in parsing writing – presumably

because they can deal better than predominantly newswire trained models can with the less canonical syntactic structures contained in the written English obtained from the web and from learners. There is no apparent difference between PCFG_WSJ_SWB_40 and PCFG_WSJ_SWB_80 (therefore the latter does no harm and we make both available), presumably because there are relatively few units greater than 40 tokens and so any performance gain here has little bearing on the overall scores. Or, CoreNLP and PCFG_WSJ_SWB_40 are able to generalise to long strings as well as the PCFG_WSJ_SWB_80 model which has been presented with long string exemplars in training.

Model	SWB	EWT	LinES	TLE
CoreNLP	.540	.744	.758	.845
PCFG_WSJ_SWB_40	.624	.748	.760	.847
PCFG_WSJ_SWB_80	.624	.748	.760	.847

Table 7: Overall unlabelled attachment scores for four English corpora and three parsing models

In Figures 3 and 4 we show the difference between the CoreNLP and PCFG models in terms of UAS delta for each input unit. These are again binned by string length, and facetted by corpus. It is apparent that the alteration for the smallest units is somewhat volatile. This is understandable

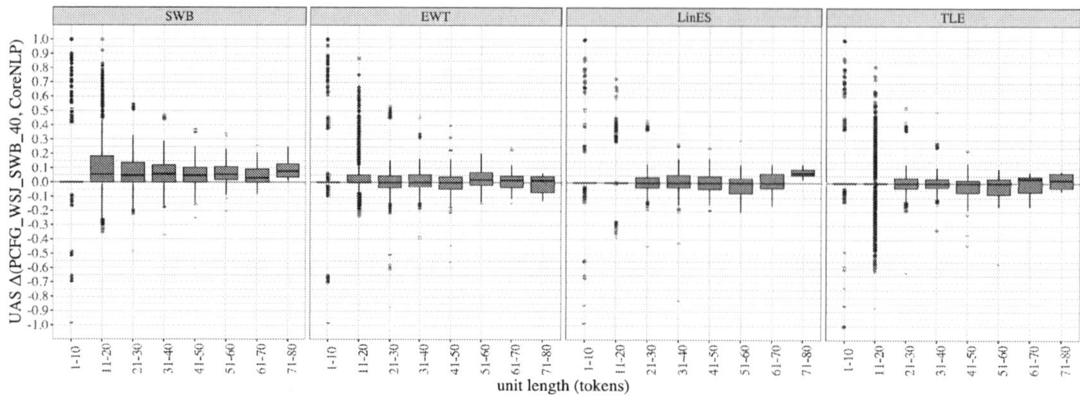

Figure 3: Unlabelled attachment scores by unit length in four English corpora: difference between model PCFG_WSJ_SWB_40 and CoreNLP.

given that a 1-token string which was correctly or incorrectly parsed by CoreNLP might now be incorrectly or correctly parsed by the PCFG models, leading to a delta of +1 or -1. Nevertheless the majority of short tokens are unaffected – shown by the median and hinges of the 1-10 token boxplot centring on y=0.

Where the added SWB training data seems to help is in units longer than 10 tokens, where the UAS delta median and hinges are consistently above zero, indicating improved performance. The boxplots tend to centre around zero for the written corpora, except for the 71-80 bin in LinES for which the boxplot is above zero, albeit for a small sample size of 5 (Table 6). The pattern for both PCFG models is broadly the same.

4   Related work

This is one among many studies examining the parsing of non-canonical data (Lease et al., 2006; Goldberg et al., 2014; Ragheb and Dickinson, 2014). Broadly speaking, there are two approaches to the problem (Eisenstein, 2013): (1) train new models specifically for non-canonical language; (2) normalise the data so that existing NLP tools work better on it. For example, Foster and colleagues (2008) deliberately introduced grammatical errors to copies of *WSJ* treebank sentences in order to train a parser to deal with noisy input. Daiber & van der Goot (2016), meanwhile, adopted the approach of text normalisation preceding syntactic parsing in dealing with social media data.

Some have proposed 'active learning' or 'self learning' algorithms for parser training, which learn from sparsely annotated or completely unannotated data (Mirroshandel and Nasr, 2011; Rei and Briscoe, 2013; Cahill et al., 2014). We could explore such methods for a speech-specific parser in future work, though they work better with large datasets to learn from – Rei & Briscoe trained on the 50 million token BLLIP corpus, for example. At the time of writing there are no similarly-sized speech corpora that we are aware of.

Relevant work on speech parsing includes that on automated disfluency detection and repair in speech transcriptions (Charniak and Johnson, 2001; Rasooli and Tetreault, 2013; Honnibal and Johnson, 2014; Moore et al., 2015; Yoshikawa et al., 2016), in which the problem has come to be addressed with a transition-based parser featuring an 'edit'-like action that can remove incrementally-constructed parse tree sections upon detection of a disfluency. Other approaches include prosodic information to detect disfluencies where the audio file is available alongside the transcription (Kahn et al., 2005). A combination of prosodic and morpho-syntactic features have been used to address another problem which affects parse quality: that of speech-unit delimitation, also known as 'speech segmentation' or 'sentence boundary detection' (Shriberg et al., 2000; Moore et al., 2016). SU delimitation and parsing were considered together as a joint problem, along with automatic speech recognition error rates, in a recent article by Kahn & Osterdorf (2012).

Finally, we should point out that we opted to work with Stanford CoreNLP for our parsing experiments because it is well-documented and well-

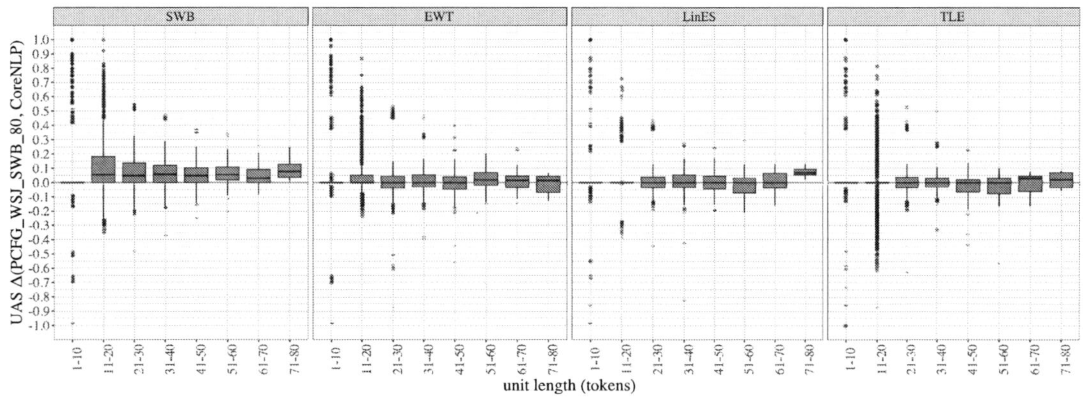

Figure 4: Unlabelled attachment scores by unit length in four English corpora: difference between model PCFG_WSJ_SWB_80 and CoreNLP.

maintained. We do not criticise the software in any way for deteriorating performance on long speech-units, as this is a hard problem, and we suspect that any other parser would suffer in similar ways. Indeed another option for future work is to use other publicly available parsers such as MSTParser (McDonald et al., 2006), TurboParser (Martins et al., 2013) and MaltParser (Nivre et al., 2007) to compare performance and potentially spot parsing errors through disagreement, per the method described by Smith & Dickinson (2014).

5 Conclusion and future work

In this paper we have shown that there are many differences between speech and writing at lexical and morphological levels. We also report how parser performance deteriorates as the input unit lengthens: an outcome which is perhaps unsurprising but which we showed to be especially acute for spoken language. Finally, we trained a new parsing model with added speech data and reported improvements for UAS scores across the board – more so for speech than writing. We make the models publicly available for other researchers[5] and welcome improved models or training data from others.

In future work we plan to analyse samples of speech-units with low UAS scores, to discover whether there are systematic parsing errors which could be solved through algorithmic changes to the parser, extra pre-processing steps, or otherwise. We also intend to continue comparing lexical and morpho-syntactic distributions in spoken and written corpora – dependency relations for example – to identify differences which may have implications for parsing. We suspect there may be lessons to be learned from parse tree analysis of learner text, such as the association between omission of the main verb and parse error (Ott and Ziai, 2010).

With more training data we can produce better parsing models, and potentially pursue self-learning algorithms in training. We might also introduce a heuristic to deal with long speech-units, which are particularly troublesome for existing parsers. One technique we can adopt is that of 'clause splitting', or 'chunking', which subdivides long strings for the purpose of higher quality analysis over small units (Tjong et al., 2001; Muszyńska, 2016). We hypothesise that such a step would play to the strength of existing parsers, namely their robustness over short inputs.

Acknowledgments

This paper reports on research supported by Cambridge English, University of Cambridge. We are grateful to our colleagues Calbert Graham and Russell Moore. We thank Sebastian Schuster and Chris Manning of Stanford University for their assistance with the Universal Dependencies corpora. We acknowledge the reviewers for their very helpful comments and have attempted to improve the paper in line with their suggestions.

---

[5] https://goo.gl/iQMu9w

References

Lars Ahrenberg. 2015. Converting an English-Swedish parallel treebank to Universal Dependencies. In *Proceedings of the Third International Conference on Dependency Linguistics (DepLing 2015)*.

Yevgeni Berzak, Jessica Kenney, Carolyn Spadine, Jing Xian Wang, Lucia Lam, Keiko Sophie Mori, Sebastian Garza, and Boris Katz. 2016. Universal Dependencies for Learner English. In *Proceedings of the 54th Annual Meeting of the Association for Computational Linguistics (Volume 1: Long Papers)*.

Douglas Biber, Stig Johansson, Geoffrey Leech, Susan Conrad, and Edward Finegan. 1999. *Longman Grammar of Spoken and Written English*. London: Longman.

Ann Bies, Justin Mott, Colin Warner, and Seth Kulick. 2012. English Web Treebank LDC2012T13.

David Brazil. 1995. *A grammar of speech*. Oxford: Oxford University Press.

Aoife Cahill, Binod Gyawali, and James Bruno. 2014. Self-training for parsing learner text. In *Proceedings of the First Joint Workshop on Statistical Parsing of Morphologically Rich Languages and Syntactic Analysis of Non-Canonical Languages*.

Andrew Caines and Paula Buttery. 2014. The effect of disfluencies and learner errors on the parsing of spoken learner language. In *Proceedings of the First Joint Workshop on Statistical Parsing of Morphologically Rich Languages and Syntactic Analysis of Non-Canonical Languages*.

Ronald Carter and Michael McCarthy. 2017. Spoken Grammar: where are we and where are we going? *Applied Linguistics* 38:1–20.

Eugene Charniak and Mark Johnson. 2001. Edit detection and parsing for transcribed speech. In *Proceedings of the 2nd Meeting of the North American Chapter of the Association for Computational Linguistics (NAACL)*. Association for Computational Linguistics.

Joachim Daiber and Rob van der Goot. 2016. The Denoised Web Treebank: evaluating dependency parsing under noisy input conditions. In *Proceedings of the Tenth International Conference on Language Resources and Evaluation (LREC)*.

Jacob Eisenstein. 2013. What to do about bad language on the internet. In *Proceedings of NAACL-HLT 2013*. Association for Computational Linguistics.

Jennifer Foster, Joachim Wagner, and Josef van Genabith. 2008. Adapting a WSJ-trained parser to grammatically noisy text. In *Proceedings of ACL-08: HLT, Short Papers*.

John J. Godfrey, Edward C. Holliman, and Jane McDaniel. 1992. Switchboard: telephone speech corpus for research and development. In *Proceedings of Acoustics, Speech, and Signal Processing (ICASSP-92)*. IEEE.

Yoav Goldberg, Yuval Marton, Ines Rehbein, Yannick Versley, Özlem Çetinoğlu, and Joel Tetreault, editors. 2014. *Proceedings of the First Joint Workshop on Statistical Parsing of Morphologically Rich Languages and Syntactic Analysis of Non-Canonical Languages*. Association for Computational Linguistics.

Matthew Honnibal and Mark Johnson. 2014. Joint incremental disfluency detection and dependency parsing. *Transactions of the Association for Computational Linguistics* 2:131–142.

Jeremy G. Kahn, Matthew Lease, Eugene Charniak, Mark Johnson, and Mari Ostendorf. 2005. Effective use of prosody in parsing conversational speech. In *Proceedings of Human Language Technology Conference and Conference on Empirical Methods in Natural Language Processing*.

Jeremy G. Kahn and Mari Ostendorf. 2012. Joint reranking of parsing and word recognition with automatic segmentation. *Computer Speech and Language* 26(1):1–19.

Dan Klein and Christopher D. Manning. 2003. Accurate unlexicalized parsing. In *Proceedings of the 41st Meeting of the Association for Computational Linguistics*.

Sandra Kübler, Ryan McDonald, and Joakim Nivre. 2009. *Dependency parsing*. Synthesis Lectures on Human Language Technologies. Morgan & Claypool Publishers.

Matthew Lease, Mark Johnson, and Eugene Charniak. 2006. Recognizing disfluencies in conversational speech. *IEEE Transactions on Audio, Speech, and Language Processing* 14:1566–1573.

Ann Lee and James Glass. 2012. Sentence detection using multiple annotations. In *Proceedings of INTERSPEECH 2012*. International Speech Communication Association.

Geoffrey Leech. 2000. Grammars of spoken English: new outcomes of corpus-oriented research. *Language Learning* 50:675–724.

William Levelt. 1989. *Speaking: from intention to articulation*. Cambridge, MA: MIT Press.

Christopher Manning, Mihai Surdeanu, John Bauer, Jenny Finkel, Steven Bethard, and David McClosky. 2014. The Stanford CoreNLP natural language processing toolkit. In *Association for Computational Linguistics (ACL) System Demonstrations*. pages 55–60.

Mitchell Marcus, Beatrice Santorini, Mary Ann Marcinkiewicz, and Ann Taylor. 1999. Treebank-3 LDC99T42.

André Martins, Miguel Almeida, and Noah Smith. 2013. Turning on the turbo: Fast third-order non-projective turbo parsers. In *Proceedings of the 51st Annual Meeting of the Association for Computational Linguistics*.

Ryan McDonald, Kevin Lerman, and Fernando Pereira. 2006. Multilingual dependency analysis with a two-stage discriminative parser. In *Proceedings of the 10th Conference on Computational Natural Language Learning (CoNLL-X)*.

Marie Meteer, Ann Taylor, Robert MacIntyre, and Rukmini Iyer. 1995. *Dysfluency annotation stylebook for the Switchboard corpus*. Philadelphia: Linguistic Data Consortium.

Seyed Mirroshandel and Alexis Nasr. 2011. Active learning for dependency parsing using partially annotated sentences. In *Proceedings of the 12th International Conference on Parsing Technologies*.

Russell Moore, Andrew Caines, Calbert Graham, and Paula Buttery. 2015. Incremental dependency parsing and disfluency detection in spoken learner English. In *Proceedings of the 18th International Conference on Text, Speech and Dialogue (TSD)*. Berlin: Springer-Verlag.

Russell Moore, Andrew Caines, Calbert Graham, and Paula Buttery. 2016. Automated speech-unit delimitation in spoken learner English. In *Proceedings of COLING*.

Ewa Muszyńska. 2016. Graph- and surface-level sentence chunking. In *Proceedings of the ACL 2016 Student Research Workshop*.

Alexis Nasr, Frederic Bechet, Benoit Favre, Thierry Bazillon, Jose Deulofeu, and Andre Valli. 2014. Automatically enriching spoken corpora with syntactic information for linguistic studies. In *Proceedings of the Ninth International Conference on Language Resources and Evaluation (LREC)*.

Joakim Nivre, Željko Agić, Lars Ahrenberg, Maria Jesus Aranzabe, Masayuki Asahara, Aitziber Atutxa, Miguel Ballesteros, John Bauer, Kepa Bengoetxea, Riyaz Ahmad Bhat, Eckhard Bick, Cristina Bosco, Gosse Bouma, Sam Bowman, Marie Candito, Gülşen Cebirolu Eryiit, Giuseppe G. A. Celano, Fabricio Chalub, Jinho Choi, Çar Çöltekin, Miriam Connor, Elizabeth Davidson, Marie-Catherine de Marneffe, Valeria de Paiva, Arantza Diaz de Ilarraza, Kaja Dobrovoljc, Timothy Dozat, Kira Droganova, Puneet Dwivedi, Marhaba Eli, Tomaž Erjavec, Richárd Farkas, Jennifer Foster, Cláudia Freitas, Katarína Gajdošová, Daniel Galbraith, Marcos Garcia, Filip Ginter, Iakes Goenaga, Koldo Gojenola, Memduh Gökrmak, Yoav Goldberg, Xavier Gómez Guinovart, Berta Gonzáles Saavedra, Matias Grioni, Normunds Grūzītis, Bruno Guillaume, Nizar Habash, Jan Hajič, Linh Hà M, Dag Haug, Barbora Hladká, Petter Hohle, Radu Ion, Elena Irimia, Anders Johannsen, Fredrik Jørgensen, Hüner Kaşkara, Hiroshi Kanayama, Jenna Kanerva, Natalia Kotsyba, Simon Krek, Veronika Laippala, Phng Lê Hng, Alessandro Lenci, Nikola Ljubešić, Olga Lyashevskaya, Teresa Lynn, Aibek Makazhanov, Christopher Manning, Cătălina Mărănduc, David Mareček, Héctor Martínez Alonso, André Martins, Jan Mašek, Yuji Matsumoto, Ryan McDonald, Anna Missilä, Verginica Mititelu, Yusuke Miyao, Simonetta Montemagni, Amir More, Shunsuke Mori, Bohdan Moskalevskyi, Kadri Muischnek, Nina Mustafina, Kaili Müürisep, Lng Nguyn Th, Huyn Nguyn Th Minh, Vitaly Nikolaev, Hanna Nurmi, Stina Ojala, Petya Osenova, Lilja Øvrelid, Elena Pascual, Marco Passarotti, Cenel-Augusto Perez, Guy Perrier, Slav Petrov, Jussi Piitulainen, Barbara Plank, Martin Popel, Lauma Pretkalnia, Prokopis Prokopidis, Tiina Puolakainen, Sampo Pyysalo, Alexandre Rademaker, Loganathan Ramasamy, Livy Real, Laura Rituma, Rudolf Rosa, Shadi Saleh, Manuela Sanguinetti, Baiba Saulīte, Sebastian Schuster, Djamé Seddah, Wolfgang Seeker, Mojgan Seraji, Lena Shakurova, Mo Shen, Dmitry Sichinava, Natalia Silveira, Maria Simi, Radu Simionescu, Katalin Simkó, Mária Šimková, Kiril Simov, Aaron Smith, Alane Suhr, Umut Sulubacak, Zsolt Szántó, Dima Taji, Takaaki Tanaka, Reut Tsarfaty, Francis Tyers, Sumire Uematsu, Larraitz Uria, Gertjan van Noord, Viktor Varga, Veronika Vincze, Jonathan North Washington, Zdeněk Žabokrtský, Amir Zeldes, Daniel Zeman, and Hanzhi Zhu. 2017. Universal Dependencies 2.0. LINDAT/CLARIN digital library at the Institute of Formal and Applied Linguistics, Charles University.

Joakim Nivre, Johan Hall, Jens Nilsson, Atanas Chanev, Gulsen Eryigit, Sandra Kübler, Svetoslav Marinov, and Erwin Marsi. 2007. MaltParser: a language-independent system for data-driven dependency parsing. *Natural Language Engineering* 13:95–135.

Niels Ott and Ramon Ziai. 2010. Evaluating dependency parsing performance on german learner language. In *Proceedings of the Ninth International Workshop on Treebanks and Linguistic Theories*.

Barbara Plank. 2016. What to do about non-standard (or *non-canonical*) language in NLP. In *Proceedings of the 13th Conference on Natural Language Processing (KONVENS 2016)*.

Marwa Ragheb and Markus Dickinson. 2014. The effect of annotation scheme decisions on parsing learner data. In *Proceedings of the 13th International Workshop on Treebanks and Linguistic Theories*.

Mohammad S. Rasooli and Joel Tetreault. 2013. Joint parsing and disfluency detection in linear time.

In *Proceedings of the 2013 Conference on Empirical Methods in Natural Language Processing (EMNLP)*. Association for Computational Linguistics.

Marek Rei and Ted Briscoe. 2013. Parser lexicalisation through self-learning. In *Proceedings of NAACL-HLT 2013*.

Elizabeth Shriberg, Andreas Stolcke, Dilek Hakkani-Tür, and Gökhan Tür. 2000. Prosody-based automatic segmentation of speech into sentences and topics. *Speech Communication* 32:127–154.

Natalia Silveira, Timothy Dozat, Marie-Catherine de Marneffe, Samuel Bowman, Miriam Connor, John Bauer, and Christopher D. Manning. 2014. A gold standard dependency corpus for English. In *Proceedings of the Ninth International Conference on Language Resources and Evaluation (LREC-2014)*.

Amber Smith and Markus Dickinson. 2014. Evaluating parse error detection across varied conditions. In *Proceedings of the 13th International Workshop on Treebanks and Linguistic Theories*.

Stephanie Strassel. 2003. *Simple metadata annotation specification*. Version 5.0.

Erik Tjong, Kim Sang, and Herv'e Déjean. 2001. Introduction to the conll-2001 shared task: Clause identification. In *Proceedings of the 2001 Workshop on Computational Natural Language Learning (CoNLL)*.

Helen Yannakoudakis, Ted Briscoe, and Ben Medlock. 2011. A new dataset and method for automatically grading ESOL texts. In *Proceedings of the 49th Annual Meeting of the Association for Computational Linguistics: Human Language Technologies-Volume 1*.

Masashi Yoshikawa, Hiroyuki Shindo, and Yuji Matsumoto. 2016. Joint transition-based dependency parsing and disfluency detection for automatic speech recognition texts. In *Proceedings of the 2016 Conference on Empirical Methods in Natural Language Processing*.

Enriching ASR Lattices with POS Tags for Dependency Parsing

Moritz Stiefel and **Ngoc Thang Vu**
Institute for Natural Language Processing (IMS)
Universität Stuttgart
Pfaffenwaldring 5B
70569 Stuttgart
{moritz.stiefel,thang.vu}@ims.uni-stuttgart.de

Abstract

Parsing speech requires a richer representation than 1-best or n-best hypotheses, e.g. lattices. Moreover, previous work shows that part-of-speech (POS) tags are a valuable resource for parsing. In this paper, we therefore explore a joint modeling approach of automatic speech recognition (ASR) and POS tagging to enrich ASR word lattices. To that end, we manipulate the ASR process from the pronouncing dictionary onward to use word-POS pairs instead of words. We evaluate ASR, POS tagging and dependency parsing (DP) performance demonstrating a successful lattice-based integration of ASR and POS tagging.

1 Introduction

Parsing speech is an essential part (Chow and Roukos, 1989; Moore et al., 1989; Su et al., 1992; Chappelier et al., 1999; Collins et al., 2004) of spoken language understanding (SLU) and difficult because spontaneous speech and syntax clash (Ehrlich and Hanrieder, 1996; Charniak and Johnson, 2001; Béchet et al., 2014). Pipeline approaches concatenating a speech recognizer, a POS tagger and a parser often rely on n-best hypotheses decoded from lattices. While n-best hypotheses cover more of the hypothesis space than the 1-best hypothesis, they are redundant and incomplete. Lattices on the other hand are efficiently representing all hypotheses under consideration and therefore allow recovery from more ASR errors. Recent work on recurrent neural network architectures with lattices as input (Ladhak et al., 2016; Su et al., 2017) promises the use of enriched lattices in SLU.

The main contribution of this work is establishing a joint ASR and POS tagging approach using the Kaldi (Povey et al., 2011) toolkit. To that end, we enrich the ASR word lattices with POS labels for all possible hypotheses on the word level. This enables subsequent natural language processing (NLP) machinery to use these syntactically richer lattices. We present our proposed method in detail including Kaldi specifics and address problems that occur when data that requires both speech and text information is used. Our results show a slight but consistent improvement of the joint model throughout the evaluations in ASR, POS tagging and DP performance.

2 Resources

We need a data resource with rich annotations for training our integrated model. Since the training process requires audio transcriptions, POS labels and gold-standard syntax annotations, all of these need to be available. Considering the general premise in data-driven methods that more data is better data, we choose the Switchboard-1 Release 2[1] (Godfrey et al., 1992) corpus with about 2400 dialogs. The Switchboard (SWBD) corpus has more recently been furnished with the NXT Switchboard annotations[2] (Calhoun et al., 2010). NXT provides a plethora of annotations and most importantly for our work, an alignment of Treebank-3[3] (Marcus et al., 1999) text and SWBD transcriptions[4]. While the Treebank-3 corpus pro-

---

[1]LDC: https://catalog.ldc.upenn.edu/LDC97S62 (Godfrey and Holliman, 1993)

[2]LDC (under CC): https://catalog.ldc.upenn.edu/LDC2009T26 (Calhoun et al., 2009)

[3]Treebank-3 at the LDC: https://catalog.ldc.upenn. edu/LDC99T42

[4]We used the corrected Mississippi State (MS-State) transcriptions: https://www.isip.piconepress.com/ projects/switchboard/

Proceedings of the First Workshop on Speech-Centric Natural Language Processing, pages 37–47
Copenhagen, Denmark, September 7–11, 2017. ©2017 Association for Computational Linguistics

vides syntax and POS tags, the transcriptions are timestamped. The alignment of these two resources offered by the NXT corpus contains all necessary annotations.

2.1 Audio

Kaldi's SWBD *s5c* recipe subsets the SWBD (LDC97S62) corpus into various training and development sets for acoustic model (AM) and language model (LM) training. For ASR evaluation, the *s5c* recipe uses a separate evaluation corpus LDC2002S09[5] of previously unreleased SWBD conversations (Linguistic Data Consortium, 2002), which was not available to us. Likewise unavailable were the Fisher corpora LDC2004T19[6] (Cieri et al., 2004) and LDC2005T19[7] (Cieri et al., 2005), which contain transcripts of conversational telephone speech for language modeling. We utilize the available SWBD data (the training set in the *s5c* recipe) and split it into training, development and evaluation set. Our results are therefore not directly comparable to other results generated from the Kaldi *s5c* recipe. We instead split our sets after the Treebank-3 splits as proposed by Charniak and Johnson (2001). This leads to less training data compared to the standard *s5c* recipe, but also yields splits common in parsing. A data summary of our SWBD splits is given in Table 1. The *lmdev* section of the SWBD corpus serves as the LM's development set and was "reserved for future use" (Charniak and Johnson, 2001, p. 121).

Set	Conv. IDs	# utt.	# tok.
train	2xxx-3xxx	90823	677160
dev	4519-4936	5697	50148
eval	4004-4153	5822	48320
lmdev	4154-4483	5949	50017

Table 1: Summary of SWBD data splits. The columns for utterances, tokens, average tokens per utterance and vocabulary depend on the choice of the transcription. These are the counts for our Treebank-3 transcription.

2.2 Transcription

While the NXT annotations provide a link between MS-State transcriptions and Treebank-3 text, we exploit this link only for the MS-State

transcription's timestamps and base our lexicon and LMs on the Treebank-3 text, rather than the MS-State transcriptions. This introduces a number of text-audio mismatches, or in other words, what is said is not what is in the annotated text. Figure 1 illustrates contractions as one characteristic difference in the tokenization of the two transcriptions: "doesn't" is represented as two tokens in the Treebank-3 data, while it is expressed as one token in the MS-State version. The second important as-

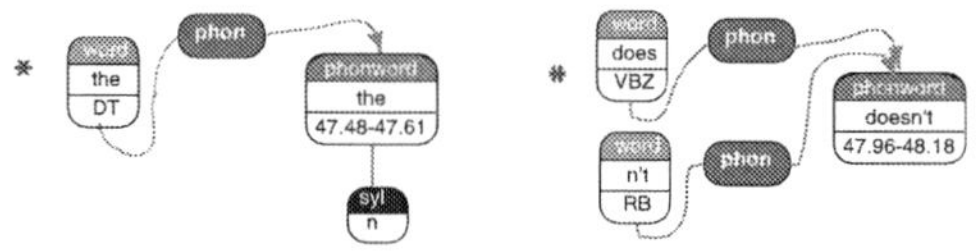

Figure 1: MS-State vs Treebank-3 transcription, from Calhoun et al. (2010, p. 392). Treebank-3 transcriptions (*word*, in light gray) are mapped to the MS-State transcriptions (*phonword* in blue) through 1-to-n relations, where multiple words in one transcription can be linked to one in the other. The box colored in black with *syl/n* in it depicts a unstressed syllable of a different annotation layer we do not consider here.

pect of choosing the Treebank-3 over the MS-State transcription, is the incongruity of utterances (cf. Calhoun et al., 2010, ch. 3.3, p. 393ff). Training and evaluation become easier if the utterances are congruent in the transcription and the Treebank-3 data with the syntactical parses. We decided to directly base the transcriptions on these annotations.

2.3 Syntax annotation

The linguistic structure annotated in the SWBD Treebank-3 section is available through the NXT Switchboard annotations and is based on the Treebank-3 text. Choosing the Treebank-3 transcription as the gold standard for the ASR system directly yields Treebank-style tokens in the recognized speech. The POS tagset (Calhoun et al., 2010, p. 394) consists of the 35 POS tags[8] in the Treebank-3 tagset. Disfluencies in the SWBD corpus are annotated following Shriberg (1994) and they are present in the Treebank-3 annotations.

3 Proposed method

First, we describe the ASR component based on the default Kaldi *s5c* recipe that generates POS-enriched word lattices in detail. Second, we introduce the POS taggers considered for the pipeline system. Third, we briefly characterize the dependency parser in our experiments.

---

[5]https://catalog.ldc.upenn.edu/LDC2002S09

[6]https://catalog.ldc.upenn.edu/LDC2004T19

[7]https://catalog.ldc.upenn.edu/LDC2005T19

[8]It is the PTB tagset without punctuation (which is covered by SYM and the remaining nine punctuation tags).

3.1 ASR with POS tagging

Starting from the *s5c* recipe, all but the acoustic modeling part underwent significant changes. The pronouncing dictionary (or lexicon), LM and resulting decoding graph now all contain word-POS pairs rather than words. We are going to outline this process step by step.

Corpus setup: Our model does not access resources other than the Switchboard-1 Release 2 (LDC97S62, with updates and corrected speaker information) data, the MS-State transcription and the Switchboard NXT corpus as described in Section 2. All transcription-based resources are being lowercased as they are in the *s5c* recipe scripts.

Transcription generation: To get a Treebank-style transcription, we query the NXT annotation corpus for pointers from MS-State tokens to Treebank-3 tokens. With this mapping, we pick the POS tags for the Treebank-3 orthography and the timestamps for the MS-State words. An example for the POS-tagged gold standard transcription is: "are|VBP you|PRP ready|JJ now|RB".

POS-enriched lexicon: We first append the lexicon with some handcrafted lexical additions for contractions of auxiliaries and adjust for tokenization differences between the source MS-State format and the target Treebank-3 format. The pronunciation of the resulting partial words is taken from the respective full entries in the dictionary supplied with the MS-State transcriptions. The lexical unit "won't", for example, is mapped to the pronunciation "w ow n t" in the MS-State version, but is not readily merged from the existing partial words ("wo" and "n't") in the MS-State lexicon and therefore is a lexical addition. Other auxiliaries, like "can't" that needs to be split as "ca n't" to conform with the Treebank-3 tokenization, and partial words in general, are added in the lexicon conversion via automated handling where all partials exist.

For all gold standard occurrences of word-POS combinations, we copy the words' pronunciations for all of the POS tags they occur with. Partial words starting with a hyphen are automatically added to the lexicon without the hyphen to account for tokenization differences. Duplicate word-POS pairs are excluded. Figure 2 shows part of the resulting POS-enriched lexicon, where "read" occurs with four different POS tags and two distinct pronunciations. We use "<unk>|XX" for unknown tokens. Note that our scheme can over-generate word-POS combinations, as it does not check whether the pronunciation variation occurs with all POS tags of a word (compare left and right parts of Figure 2).

```
read|VB  r eh d
read|VB  r iy d
read|VBD r eh d
read|VBD r iy d
read|VBN r eh d
read|VBN r iy d
read|VBP r eh d       read r eh d
read|VBP r iy d       read r iy d
```

Figure 2: Pronunciation entries for "read" in the lexicon, with (left) and without (right) POS tags.

Language modeling: LM training is performed on the *train* set with the *lmdev* set as heldout data. We train the LM on the POS-enriched transcription directly. See Figure 3 for example trigrams.

```
-0.000432954    we|PRP ca|MD n't|RB
-0.0004147099   's|BES kind|RB of|RB
-0.0003858729   they|PRP ca|MD n't|RB
-0.0002859116   just|RB kind|RB of|RB
-0.0001056216   you|PRP ca|MD n't|RB
```

Figure 3: Top 5 trigrams in the Joint-LM, based on the conditional log probabilities in the first column.

Different from the *s5c* recipe, we compute trigram and bigram LMs with SRILM[9] (Stolcke, 2002) and "<unk>|XX" as unknown token. As discussed in Section 2, we did not use SWBD-external resources for mixing and interpolating our LMs. We use SRILM with modified Kneser-Ney smoothing (Chen and Goodman, 1999) with interpolated estimates, and use only words occurring in the specified vocabulary and not in the count files. We report LM perplexity (PPL) on the *lmdev* held-out data in Table 2. Note that the joint model LM in Table 2 encounters 150 OOV tokens (e.g. hyphenated numerals like "thirty-seven"). The PPLs increase slightly for the joint model because the vocabulary has n entries for each word, where n is the number of POS tags the word occurs with.

Acoustic modeling: We use the original *s5c* recipe and only adjust the training, development and evaluation splits after Charniak and Johnson (2001) (cf. Table 1). None of the other aforementioned adaptations are applied and the manually corrected MS-State transcriptions are in use. The *tri4* model in the *s5c* recipe is a triphone

---

[9] http://www.speech.sri.com/projects/srilm/

LM	PPL
Baseline 2-gram	89.4
Baseline 3-gram	76.3
Joint 2-gram	96.4
Joint 3-gram	84.2

Table 2: PPL and OOVs on *lmdev*.

(with one context phone to the left and right) model which was trained with speaker-adaptive training (SAT, Anastasakos et al., 1996; Povey et al., 2008) technique using feature-space maximum likelihood linear regression (fMLLR, Gales, 1998). We train this *tri4* AM on the training split in Table 1 with duplicate utterances removed.

3.2 Baseline POS tagging

We perform POS tagging with three out-of-the-box taggers, two of them with pretrained models, and choose the best one for our baseline pipeline model.

NLTK's (Bird et al., 2009) former default maximum entropy-based (ME) POS tagger with the pretrained model trained on WSJ data from the PTB (for an overview, see Taylor et al., 2003) is the first tagger and we term it *ME.pre*. We also train a ME POS tagger[10] that is implemented after Ratnaparkhi (1996) on the first 70,000 sentences[11] of our SWBD training split, described in Section 2, and denote our self-trained model by *ME.70k*. We configure the ME classifier to use the optimized version of MEGAM (Daumé III, 2004) for speed.

The second tagger is NLTK's current default tagger, based on a greedy averaged perceptron (AP) tagger developed by Matthew Honnibal[12]. We name the AP tagger with the pretrained NLTK model *AP.pre*, and the same tagger trained on the full training split *AP*.

To have an NLTK-external industry-standard POS tagger in our comparison, we also run spaCy's POS tagger (see `https://spacy.io/`, we used spaCy in version 1.0.3) with its pretrained English model (also trained with AP learning).

---

[10]Available in NLTK and at: `https://github.com/arne-cl/nltk-maxent-pos-tagger`

[11]The sentences are sorted by their utterance id. The full training set was not computationally feasible: MEGAM threw an "out of memory" error.

[12]`https://explosion.ai/blog/part-of-speech-pos-tagger-in-python`

3.3 Dependency parsing

In this work, we compare dependency parsing results of (a) the 1-best hypothesis of the baseline *tri4* ASR system with the self-trained AP POS tagger and (b) the 1-best hypotheses of our joint model. We use a greedy neural-based dependency parser reimplemented after the greedy baseline in Weiss et al. (2015).

The parser's training set is the gold standard data of the training split and identical for the *tri4* and the Joint-POS model with 62728 trainable sentences out of 63304 (= 99.09%). In this evaluation, we tune the parser based on development data and use word- and POS-based features. The parser implementation uses averaged stochastic gradient descent proposed independently by Ruppert (1988) and Polyak and Juditsky (1992) with momentum (Rumelhart et al., 1986). We do not embed any external information.

4 Results

Our evaluation includes intermediate ASR and POS tagging results and a DP-based evaluation. We evaluate partially correct ASR hypotheses with a simplistic scoring method that allows imprecise scoring when the recognized sequence of tokens does not match the gold standard.

4.1 ASR

We test our joint ASR and POS model against the default *tri4* model in a ASR-only evaluation of the 1-best hypotheses. As we generate the word-POS pairs jointly and they are part of the ASR hypotheses, we strip the POS tags for the word-only evaluation in Table 3. We evaluate the ASR step based on word error rate (WER) and sentence error rate (SER).

Set	Default *tri4*	Joint-POS
dev	**28.75** (65.83)	28.93 (**65.28**)
eval	29.41 (64.41)	**29.26 (64.15)**

Table 3: ASR results: numbers are WER (SER) as percentages. POS tags stripped when evaluating joint model.

Recall that these results are not directly comparable to other ASR results on the SWBD corpus, because of our data splits with less training data and use of the Treebank-3 transcription. In the unaltered (apart from the splits, see Section 2.1), original *s5c* recipe, the WER on the *eval* set with the original MS-State transcriptions (48926 tokens, 4331 utterances) is 26.51% with a SER of 67.91%. Compared to the baseline, the results of our Joint-POS model are slightly better for the *dev* set and *eval* set in SER, and for the *eval* set also in WER.

4.2 POS tagging

We present an evaluation of our joint model's performance up to the baseline model's POS tagging step. We compare against the POS tagger performance on the 1-best ASR hypotheses in the pipeline approach. As the 1-best hypotheses of joint and pipeline model can differ, we evaluate the POS tagging step on ASR output against the word-POS pair Treebank-3 gold standard by means of WER.

Tagger	dev	eval
ME.pre	43.29 (94.23)	44.49 (94.19)
AP.pre	45.46 (95.84)	46.18 (95.74)
spaCy.pre	39.17 (82.83)	40.42 (81.86)
ME.70k	33.24 (68.18)	36.35 (54.98)
AP	32.30 (67.67)	33.10 (66.85)
Joint-POS	**32.05 (67.32)**	**32.52 (66.52)**

Table 4: POS tagging results: numbers are WER (SER) on the 1-best hypotheses. ME.70k is trained on the first 70,000 training set sentences. A model name ending in *.pre* indicates the use of a pretrained model. Model names without dotted endings are trained on the full SWBD training set. Best scores per set are in boldface.

Table 4 shows that the Joint-POS model consistently outperforms the baseline POS taggers on both sets. The pretrained models clearly have not been trained on speech data and unsurprisingly perform poorly. Our self-trained ME and AP models improve at least 6% in WER and 15% in SER over the pretrained models. The margin by which our joint model surpasses the self-trained AP tagger is small with an improvement of 0.25% WER on the *dev* and 0.58% WER on the *eval* set. The self-trained AP tagger performed best of the baseline taggers and we therefore use it in for the DP-based evaluation in the next section.

4.3 DP

We evaluate our joint ASR-POS model on the target task by running a dependency parser on POS-tagged 1-best hypotheses. In the competing pipeline model, we score the output of the default

tri4 ASR 1-best hypotheses tagged by the AP tagger we trained ourselves. All results in Table 5 and Table 6 show that our joint model does profit from the joint ASR and POS modeling in our approach.

Set	#utts	#tokens	*tri4* UAS	*tri4* LAS	Joint-POS UAS	Joint-POS LAS
dev	900	4881	94.30	92.71	**95.41**	**93.63**
eval	882	4827	94.68	93.06	**94.92**	**93.52**
dev_P	942	5261	94.16	92.38	—	—
$eval_P$	921	5134	94.06	92.31	—	—
dev_J	932	5158	—	—	94.65	92.88
$eval_J$	921	5137	—	—	94.61	92.93

Table 5: Parsing results for subsets of correct tokenizations. Labeled attachment scores (LAS) and unlabeled attachment scores (UAS) given as percentages. Best scores on the common sets in boldface.

Table 5 features evaluations of six different development and evaluation sets. The sets named *dev* and *eval* are the common subsets of token-level correct hypotheses that the pipeline and joint model share and therefore can be directly compared on. The sets indexed with a P or J are the token-level correct hypotheses for the pipeline and joint model respectively. As the models are not identical with respect to their 1-best hypotheses that match the Treebank-3 data, we also present the results using all available correctly tokenized ASR hypotheses. Our Joint-POS model consistently outperforms the pipeline *tri4* approach between 1.11% (*dev*, UAS) and 0.24% (*eval*, UAS) on the common subsets. The results are similar for the non-matching subsets. Note, that the results in Table 5 are for the small subset of utterances with a correct token sequence, i.e. where the (converted and filtered) Treebank-3 sentence tokens match the ASR hypothesis words exactly. This restriction allows an evaluation with LAS and UAS because the tokenization is identical and we have gold data for this correct token sequence. To (a) have a more extensive evaluation on all the utterances we have hypotheses for[13] and (b) be able to compare the pipeline and joint approach on the hypotheses coverage and close misses of the correct tokenization, too, we present Table 6.

We cannot use the standard parsing evaluation measures that depend on a correct word sequence to get scores on imperfectly recognized utterances.

---

[13] There are a few empty utterances with negligible counts.

We address this problem with a simple but imprecise solution: (1.) Parse the development and evaluation set using the parser models previously trained and tuned on the common sets (see Table 5); (2.) Evaluate the parser predictions on the ASR hypotheses against the gold Treebank-3 data with a imprecise scoring method that allows for a mismatch of the gold and predicted token sequence. We introduce two simple scores, unlabeled score (US) and labeled score (LS), with their names derived from UAS and LAS respectively (see Table 6). Recall that UAS requires a relation's head and dependent to match including their position and LAS requires a matching label (or dependency type) on that relation in addition.

The imprecision in the US and LS scoring stems from ignoring the positions of head and dependent in the utterance completely. We iterate over the utterances and for every token (or dependent) look up its head (word) and count this relation as a US match if the lookup is successful. When there is a US match, we also check for a matching label and count that as an LS match. The US and LS counts are normalized by the number of tokens in the Treebank-3 reference. The improvement our Joint-POS model shows over the pipeline *tri4* model is small for all scores, but consistent.

Model	Set	UAS	LAS	US	LS
tri4	dev	32.20	31.20	52.02	49.40
	eval	31.21	30.29	50.72	48.33
Joint-POS	dev	**32.41**	**31.43**	**52.21**	**49.71**
	eval	**31.56**	**30.73**	**51.21**	**48.99**

Table 6: Parsing results on full *dev* and *eval* sets. LAS, UAS, LS and US are given as percentages. The *dev* set has 3994 utterances with 44760 tokens and the *eval* set has 3912 utterances with 43277 tokens. Best scores per set in boldface.

5 DP-based analysis

We tentatively analyze in which cases the joint model does better than the pipeline approach. We first give absolute counts for how often this is the case in Table 7. While the Joint-POS model receives higher counts for all scores, there are also a considerable number of cases where the pipeline model makes fewer mistakes. We pick all examples randomly from the instances counted in the *All* column of Table 7 and focus on short sentences for presentability.

Model	UAS	LAS	US	LS	All
tri4	320	330	483	496	233
Joint-POS	332	363	540	596	267

Table 7: Utterance-based parsing evaluation. The numbers are counts of utterances where the model in the first column is better than the other. Column *All* gives the counts for when it is better on all four measures.

In the following examples, we highlight the important differences in boldface. In Figure 4, we see a fully correct Joint-POS model. While the pipeline approach does also recognize the correct word sequence, a POS tagging error causes the parsing to be erroneous on two arcs. This error affects all four scores (UAS, LAS, US and LS), as the parsing model not only misclassifies the label, but also attaches the head of "there" incorrectly. We visualize the error's effect in a correct vs incorrect tree comparison.

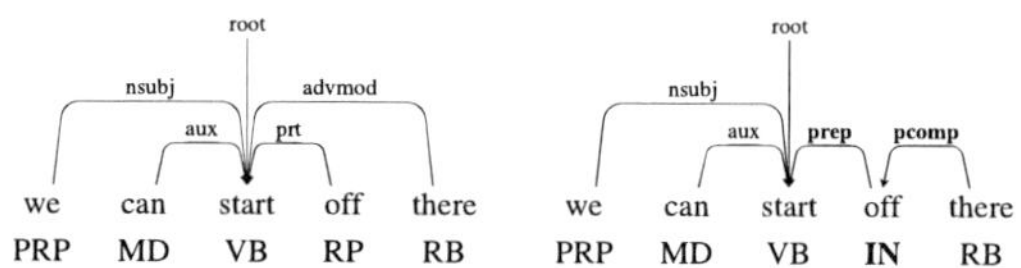

Figure 4: Dependency graph comparison #1. Correct Joint-POS tree on the left, incorrect *tri4* tree on the right.

We observe a recognition error in the pipeline *tri4* model that causes a different reading and syntactical structure in Figure 5. While it is acceptable spontaneous speech (e.g. "I like rock.. and like some country music."), "and" would not be the subject of the sentence.

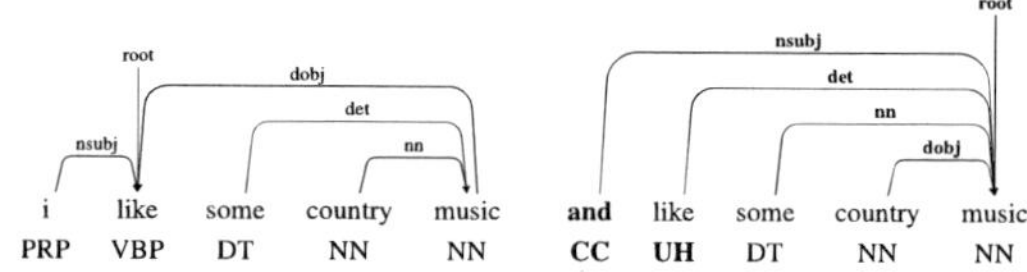

Figure 5: Dependency graph comparison #2. Correct Joint-POS tree on the left, incorrect *tri4* tree on the right.

The third graph visualization in Figure 6 illustrates an ASR deletion error on the first word. The pipeline *tri4* model handles the error gracefully, but receives lower US and LS scores because of the token mismatch nonetheless. If we had not allowed the imprecise evaluation, we would not have observed this kind of error.

The example in Figure 7 also has an ASR error in the pipeline approach at its core. In this case,

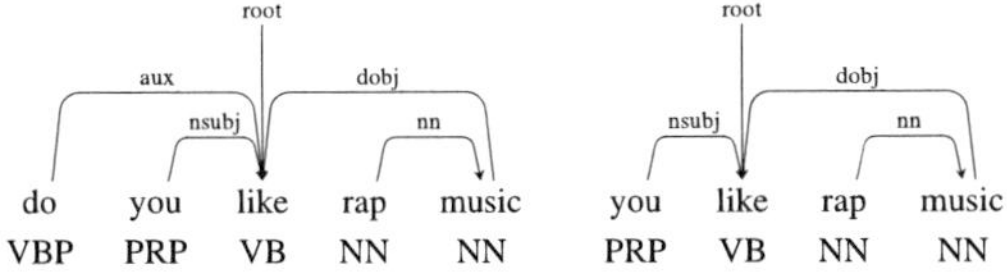

Figure 6: Dependency graph comparison #3. Correct Joint-POS tree on the left, incorrect *tri4* tree on the right.

while the joint model is entirely correct, the recognition error in the pipeline causes two POS tagging errors resulting in an incorrect parse.

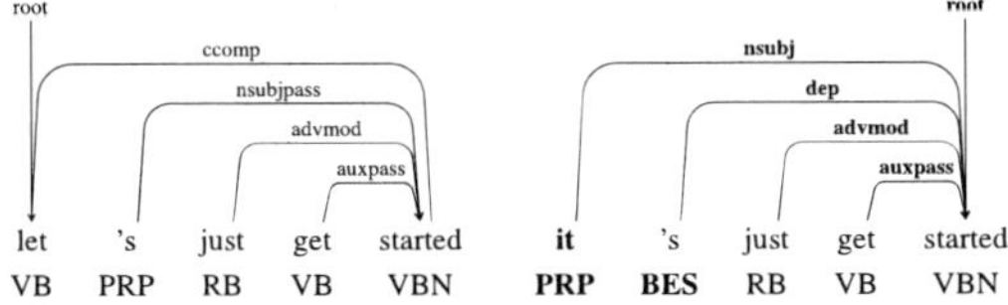

Figure 7: Dependency graph comparison #4. Correct Joint-POS tree on the left, incorrect *tri4* tree on the right.

The example utterance in Table 8 contains ASR errors in the both models' hypotheses with subsequent errors in POS tagging and parsing. We can glean that discourse interjections like "uh.. uh.." can be misrecognized as regular words, an error characteristic of spontaneous speech. Note, that the joint model gets the word "families" right, but as an object instead the subject. The pipeline model produces four word errors in sequence and "families" does not appear in its hypothesis.

6   Related work

Spoken language poses a variety of problems for NLP. The recognition of spoken language can suffer from poor recording equipment, noisy environments, unclear speech or speech pathologies. It also exhibits spontaneity, ungrammaticality and disfluencies, e.g. repairs and restarts (cf. Shriberg (1994)). Hence, in addition to ASR errors, downstream tasks such as parsing have to deal with these difficulties of conversational speech, whether the ASR output is in the form of n-best sequences or lattices. Jørgensen (2007) remove disfluencies prior to parsing and find their removal improves the performance of both a dependency and a head-driven lexicalized statistical parser on SWBD. In a more general joint approach of disfluency detection and DP, Honnibal and Johnson (2014) in contrast to Jørgensen (2007) make use of the disfluency annotations and report strong results for both, disfluency annota-

tion and DP. Rasooli and Tetreault (2013) extend the arc-eager transition system (Nivre, 2008) with actions that handle reparanda, discourse markers and interjections, thereby also explicitly using marked disfluencies on SWBD for joint DP and disfluency detection. Where Rasooli and Tetreault (2013) and Honnibal and Johnson (2014) work with SWBD text data, Yoshikawa et al. (2016) are close to our setting and assume ASR output text as parser input. Yoshikawa et al. (2016) create an alignment that enables the transfer of gold treebank data to ASR output texts and add three actions to manage disfluencies and ASR errors to the arc-eager shift-reduce transition system of Zhang and Nivre (2011). While they do not parse lattices or confusion networks (lattices can be converted to confusion networks, see Mangu et al. (2000)) directly, Yoshikawa et al. (2016) use information from word confusion networks to discover erroneous regions in the ASR output. Charniak and Johnson (2001) parse SWBD after removing edited speech that they identify with a linear classifier. Additionally, Charniak and Johnson (2001) introduce a *relaxed edited* parsing metric that considers a simplified gold standard constituent parse (removed edited words are added back into the constituent parse for evaluation). Johnson and Charniak (2004) model speech repairs in a noisy channel model utilizing tree adjoining grammars (TAGs). Source sentence probabilities in the noisy channel are computed with a bigram LM and rescored with a syntactic parser for a more global view on the source sentence. The noisy channel is then formalized as TAG that maps source sentences to target sentences, where repairs are treated as the cleaned target side of the reparanda on the source side. Besides the words themselves, Johnson and Charniak (2004) use POS tags for the alignment of reparandum and repair, which indicates their usefulness in detecting disfluencies. Approaching spontaneous speech issues from another angle, Béchet et al. (2014) adapt a parser trained on written text by means of an interactive web interface (Bazillon et al., 2012) in which users can modify POS and dependency tags writing regular expressions.

Natural speech poses specific problems, but also comes with acoustic information that can improve parsing speech through its incorporation (Tran et al., 2017) or reranking (Kahn et al., 2005). Handling disfluencies following Charniak and Johnson

ID	Treebank-3				Joint-POS				tri4			
	Word	POS	Head	Dep.	Word	POS	Head	Dep.	Word	POS	Head	Dep.
1	well	UH	7	discourse	well	UH	7	discourse	well	UH	**0**	**root**
2	how	WRB	3	advmod	how	WRB	3	advmod	how	WRB	3	advmod
3	many	JJ	6	amod	many	JJ	**7**	**nsubj**	many	JJ	**1**	**dep**
4	uh	UH	6	discourse	**of**	**IN**	**3**	**dep**	**of**	**IN**	3	**dep**
5	uh	UH	6	discourse	**of**	**IN**	3	**prep**	**of**	**IN**	3	**prep**
6	families	NNS	7	nsubj	families	NNS	5	pobj	**own**	NNS	5	pobj
7	own	VBP	0	root	**own**	**VB**	0	root	**on**	**IN**	3	**prep**
8	a	DT	9	det	a	DT	9	det	a	DT	9	det
9	refrigerator	NN	7	dobj	refrigerator	NN	7	dobj	refrigerator	NN	7	**pobj**

Table 8: Example utterance. Errors in both models in boldface.

(2001), Kahn et al. (2005) rerank the n-best parses using a set of prosodic features in the reranking framework of Collins (2000). Kahn et al. (2005) find that combining prosodic features with non-local syntactic features increase F-scores in the relaxed edited metric of Charniak and Johnson (2001). Kahn and Ostendorf (2012) present an approach that automatically recognizes speech, segments a stream of words (e.g. a conversation side/speaker turn) into sentences and parses these. A reranker that can take into account ASR posteriors for n-best ASR hypotheses as well as parse-specific features for m-best parses can then jointly optimize towards WER (n hypotheses) or SParseval (Roark et al., 2006) ($n \times m$ hypotheses) metrics (Kahn and Ostendorf, 2012). Ehrlich and Hanrieder (1996) describe an agenda-driven chart parser that considers an acoustic word-level score from a word lattice and can combine a sentence-spanning analysis from partial hypotheses if a full parse is unobtainable. Tran et al. (2017) use speech and text domain cues for constituent parsing in an attention-based encoder-decoder approach based on Vinyals et al. (2015). They show that word-level acoustic-prosodic features learned with convolutional neural networks improve performance.

7 Discussion

Replacing words with word-POS pairs throughout the ASR process, as described in Section 3.1, increases the search space considerably. We focus on establishing the feasibility of this approach here and do not detail techniques to address this complexity issue. Including prior distributions of word-POS pair occurrences could help disambiguation early on in lattice creation. The LM in the joint model relies on word-POS pairs as well,

and a smoothing approach that backs off to n-grams of words instead of n-grams of word-POS pairs would counter the increased sparsity due to the combination of words and their POS tags in the LM part. We only explore instances of errors the joint and pipeline models make in our analysis. A systematic error analysis identifying advantages and disadvantages of the joint model would be interesting, especially with the errors involving contractions and disfluencies. As a negative example for our joint model, we observed the separation of "didn't" as "did" plus "n't" as an ASR error for "did it". A qualitative analysis of error types could indicate whether this a random or systematic error, and the same is true of the positive examples in Section 5.

8 Conclusion

We have demonstrated a method to jointly perform POS tagging and ASR on speech. The tagging and parsing evaluations of the pipeline model vs our joint model confirm the successful integration of POS tags into speech lattices. While the improvements over the pipeline approach are small, we enrich lattices with POS tags that allow for latticed-based NLP in future work.

Acknowledgments

We thank the anonymous reviewers for their extensive and helpful feedback on this work. We also thank Xiang Yu for his parser implementation and Wolfgang Seeker for helping with the conversion to dependency parses. This work was funded by the German Research Foundation (DFG) through the Collaborative Research Center (SFB) 732, project A8, at the University of Stuttgart.

References

Tasos Anastasakos, John Mcdonough, Richard Schwartz, and John Makhoul. 1996. A compact model for speaker-adaptive training. In *Proc. ICSLP*, pages 1137–1140.

Thierry Bazillon, Melanie Deplano, Frederic Bechet, Alexis Nasr, and Benoit Favre. 2012. Syntactic annotation of spontaneous speech: application to call-center conversation data. In *Proceedings of the Eight International Conference on Language Resources and Evaluation (LREC'12)*, Istanbul, Turkey. European Language Resources Association (ELRA).

Frédéric Béchet, Alexis Nasr, and Benoît Favre. 2014. Adapting dependency parsing to spontaneous speech for open domain spoken language understanding. In *INTERSPEECH 2014, 15th Annual Conference of the International Speech Communication Association, Singapore, September 14-18, 2014*, pages 135–139. ISCA.

Steven Bird, Ewan Klein, and Edward Loper. 2009. *Natural Language Processing with Python*. O'Reilly.

Sasha Calhoun, Jean Carletta, Jason M. Brenier, Neil Mayo, Dan Jurafsky, Mark Steedman, and David Beaver. 2010. The NXT-format switchboard corpus: a rich resource for investigating the syntax, semantics, pragmatics and prosody of dialogue. *Language Resources and Evaluation*, 44(4):387–419.

Sasha Calhoun, Jean Carletta, Daniel Jurafsky, Malvina Nissim, Mari Ostendorf, and Annie Zaenen. 2009. NXT switchboard annotations LDC2009T26. Web Download.

J.-C. Chappelier, M. Rajman, R. Aragüés, and A. Rozenknop. 1999. Lattice parsing for speech recognition. In *Proc. of 6ème conférence sur le Traitement Automatique du Langage Naturel (TALN99)*, pages 95–104, Cargèse (France).

Eugene Charniak and Mark Johnson. 2001. Edit detection and parsing for transcribed speech. In *Proceedings of the second meeting of the North American Chapter of the Association for Computational Linguistics on Language technologies*, pages 118–126. Association for Computational Linguistics.

Stanley F. Chen and Joshua Goodman. 1999. An empirical study of smoothing techniques for language modeling. *Computer Speech & Language*, 13(4):359–393.

Yen-Lu Chow and Salim Roukos. 1989. Speech understanding using a unification grammar. In *Acoustics, Speech, and Signal Processing, 1989. ICASSP-89., 1989 International Conference on*, pages 727–730 vol.2.

Christopher Cieri, David Graff, Owen Kimball, Dave Miller, and Kevin Walker. 2004. Fisher english training speech part 1 transcripts LDC2004T19. Web Download.

Christopher Cieri, David Graff, Owen Kimball, Dave Miller, and Kevin Walker. 2005. Fisher english training speech part 2, transcripts LDC2005T19. Web Download.

Christopher Collins, Bob Carpenter, and Gerald Penn. 2004. Head-driven parsing for word lattices. In *Proceedings of the 42nd Annual Meeting of the Association for Computational Linguistics, 21-26 July, 2004, Barcelona, Spain.*, pages 231–238. ACL.

Michael Collins. 2000. Discriminative reranking for natural language parsing. In *Proceedings of the Seventeenth International Conference on Machine Learning (ICML 2000), Stanford University, Stanford, CA, USA, June 29 - July 2, 2000*, pages 175–182. Morgan Kaufmann.

Hal Daumé III. 2004. Notes on CG and LM-BFGS optimization of logistic regression. Paper available at http://pub.hal3.name#daume04cg-bfgs, implementation available at http://hal3.name/megam/.

Ute Ehrlich and Gerhard Hanrieder. 1996. Robust speech parsing. In *Proceedings of the Eight European Summer School In Logic, Language and Information*.

M.J.F. Gales. 1998. Maximum likelihood linear transformations for hmm-based speech recognition. *Computer Speech & Language*, 12(2):75–98.

John Godfrey and Edward Holliman. 1993. Switchboard-1 release 2 LDC97S62. Web Download.

John J. Godfrey, Edward C. Holliman, and Jane McDaniel. 1992. Switchboard: Telephone speech corpus for research and development. In *Proceedings of the 1992 IEEE International Conference on Acoustics, Speech and Signal Processing - Volume 1*, ICASSP'92, pages 517–520, Washington, DC, USA. IEEE Computer Society.

Matthew Honnibal and Mark Johnson. 2014. Joint incremental disfluency detection and dependency parsing. *TACL*, 2:131–142.

Mark Johnson and Eugene Charniak. 2004. A tag-based noisy-channel model of speech repairs. In *Proceedings of the 42nd Annual Meeting of the Association for Computational Linguistics, 21-26 July, 2004, Barcelona, Spain.*, pages 33–39. ACL.

Fredrik Jørgensen. 2007. The effects of disfluency detection in parsing spoken language. In *Proceedings of the 16th Nordic Conference of Computational Linguistics NODALIDA-2007*, pages 240–244.

Jeremy G. Kahn, Matthew Lease, Eugene Charniak, Mark Johnson, and Mari Ostendorf. 2005. Effective use of prosody in parsing conversational speech.

In *Proceedings of the Conference on Human Language Technology and Empirical Methods in Natural Language Processing*, HLT '05, pages 233–240, Stroudsburg, PA, USA. Association for Computational Linguistics.

Jeremy G. Kahn and Mari Ostendorf. 2012. Joint reranking of parsing and word recognition with automatic segmentation. *Computer Speech & Language*, 26(1):1–19.

Faisal Ladhak, Ankur Gandhe, Markus Dreyer, Lambert Mathias, Ariya Rastrow, and Björn Hoffmeister. 2016. Latticernn: Recurrent neural networks over lattices. In *Interspeech 2016*, pages 695–699.

Linguistic Data Consortium. 2002. 2000 hub5 english evaluation speech LDC2002S09. Web Download.

Lidia Mangu, Eric Brill, and Andreas Stolcke. 2000. Finding consensus in speech recognition: word error minimization and other applications of confusion networks. *Computer Speech & Language*, 14(4):373–400.

Mitchell Marcus, Beatrice Santorini, Mary Ann Marcinkiewicz, and Ann Taylor. 1999. Treebank-3 LDC99T42. Web Download.

Robert Moore, Fernando Pereira, and Hy Murveit. 1989. Integrating speech and natural-language processing. In *Proceedings of the Workshop on Speech and Natural Language*, HLT '89, pages 243–247, Stroudsburg, PA, USA. Association for Computational Linguistics.

Joakim Nivre. 2008. Algorithms for deterministic incremental dependency parsing. *Comput. Linguist.*, 34(4):513–553.

B. T. Polyak and A. B. Juditsky. 1992. Acceleration of stochastic approximation by averaging. *SIAM Journal on Control and Optimization*, 30(4):838–855.

Daniel Povey, Arnab Ghoshal, Gilles Boulianne, Lukas Burget, Ondrej Glembek, Nagendra Goel, Mirko Hannemann, Petr Motlicek, Yanmin Qian, Petr Schwarz, Jan Silovsky, Georg Stemmer, and Karel Vesely. 2011. The kaldi speech recognition toolkit. In *IEEE 2011 Workshop on Automatic Speech Recognition and Understanding*. IEEE Signal Processing Society. IEEE Catalog No.: CFP11SRW-USB.

Daniel Povey, Hong-Kwang Jeff Kuo, and Hagen Soltau. 2008. Fast speaker adaptive training for speech recognition. In *INTERSPEECH 2008, 9th Annual Conference of the International Speech Communication Association, Brisbane, Australia, September 22-26, 2008*, pages 1245–1248. ISCA.

Mohammad Sadegh Rasooli and Joel Tetreault. 2013. Joint parsing and disfluency detection in linear time. In *Proceedings of the 2013 Conference on Empirical Methods in Natural Language Processing*, pages 124–129, Seattle, Washington, USA. Association for Computational Linguistics.

Adwait Ratnaparkhi. 1996. A maximum entropy model for part-of-speech tagging. In *Proceedings of the Conference on Empirical Methods in Natural Language Processing*, volume 1, pages 133–142. Philadelphia, USA.

B. Roark, M. Harper, E. Charniak, B. Dorr, M. Johnson, J. Kahn, Y. Liu, M. Ostendorf, J. Hale, A. Krasnyanskaya, M. Lease, I. Shafran, M. Snover, R. Stewart, and L. Yung. 2006. Sparseval: Evaluation metrics for parsing speech. In *Proceedings of the Fifth International Conference on Language Resources and Evaluation (LREC'06)*. European Language Resources Association (ELRA).

David E. Rumelhart, Geoffrey E. Hinton, and Ronald J. Williams. 1986. Learning representations by back-propagating errors. *Nature*, 323(6088):533–536.

David Ruppert. 1988. Efficient estimations from a slowly convergent robbins-monro process. Technical Report 781, Cornell University Operations Research and Industrial Engineering.

Elizabeth Ellen Shriberg. 1994. *Preliminaries to a Theory of Speech Disfluencies*. Ph.D. thesis, University of California at Berkeley.

Andreas Stolcke. 2002. SRILM - an extensible language modeling toolkit. In *7th International Conference on Spoken Language Processing, IC-SLP2002 - INTERSPEECH 2002, Denver, Colorado, USA, September 16-20, 2002*. ISCA.

Jinsong Su, Zhixing Tan, Deyi Xiong, Rongrong Ji, Xiaodong Shi, and Yang Liu. 2017. Lattice-based recurrent neural network encoders for neural machine translation. In *Proceedings of the Thirty-First AAAI Conference on Artificial Intelligence, February 4-9, 2017, San Francisco, California, USA.*, pages 3302–3308. AAAI Press.

Keh-Yih Su, Tung-Hui Chiang, and Yi-Chung Lin. 1992. A unified framework to incorporate speech and language information in spoken language processing. In *Acoustics, Speech, and Signal Processing, 1992. ICASSP-92., 1992 IEEE International Conference on*, volume 1, pages 185–188 vol.1.

Ann Taylor, Mitchell Marcus, and Beatrice Santorini. 2003. The penn treebank: An overview. In Anne Abeillé, editor, *Treebanks: Building and Using Parsed Corpora*, pages 5–22. Springer Netherlands, Dordrecht.

Trang Tran, Shubham Toshniwal, Mohit Bansal, Kevin Gimpel, Karen Livescu, and Mari Ostendorf. 2017. Joint modeling of text and acoustic-prosodic cues for neural parsing. *CoRR*, abs/1704.07287.

Oriol Vinyals, Lukasz Kaiser, Terry Koo, Slav Petrov, Ilya Sutskever, and Geoffrey E. Hinton. 2015. Grammar as a foreign language. In *Advances in Neural Information Processing Systems 28: Annual Conference on Neural Information Processing Systems 2015, December 7-12, 2015, Montreal, Quebec, Canada*, pages 2773–2781.

David Weiss, Chris Alberti, Michael Collins, and Slav Petrov. 2015. Structured training for neural network transition-based parsing. In *Proceedings of the 53rd Annual Meeting of the Association for Computational Linguistics and the 7th International Joint Conference on Natural Language Processing of the Asian Federation of Natural Language Processing, ACL 2015, July 26-31, 2015, Beijing, China, Volume 1: Long Papers*, pages 323–333. The Association for Computer Linguistics.

Masashi Yoshikawa, Hiroyuki Shindo, and Yuji Matsumoto. 2016. Joint transition-based dependency parsing and disfluency detection for automatic speech recognition texts. In *Proceedings of the 2016 Conference on Empirical Methods in Natural Language Processing, EMNLP 2016, Austin, Texas, USA, November 1-4, 2016*, pages 1036–1041. The Association for Computational Linguistics.

Yue Zhang and Joakim Nivre. 2011. Transition-based dependency parsing with rich non-local features. In *The 49th Annual Meeting of the Association for Computational Linguistics: Human Language Technologies, Proceedings of the Conference, 19-24 June, 2011, Portland, Oregon, USA - Short Papers*, pages 188–193. The Association for Computer Linguistics.

End-to-End Information Extraction without Token-Level Supervision

Rasmus Berg Palm
DTU Compute
Technical University of Denmark
rapal@dtu.dk

Dirk Hovy
Computer Science Dpeartment
University of Copenhagen
dirk.hovy@di.ku.dk

Florian Laws
Tradeshift
Landemærket 10, 1119 Copenhagen
fla@tradeshift.com

Ole Winther
DTU Compute
Technical University of Denmark
olwi@dtu.dk

Abstract

Most state-of-the-art information extraction approaches rely on token-level labels to find the areas of interest in text. Unfortunately, these labels are time-consuming and costly to create, and consequently, not available for many real-life IE tasks. To make matters worse, token-level labels are usually not the desired output, but just an intermediary step. End-to-end (E2E) models, which take raw text as input and produce the desired output directly, need not depend on token-level labels. We propose an E2E model based on pointer networks, which can be trained directly on pairs of raw input and output text. We evaluate our model on the ATIS data set, MIT restaurant corpus and the MIT movie corpus and compare to neural baselines that do use token-level labels. We achieve competitive results, within a few percentage points of the baselines, showing the feasibility of E2E information extraction without the need for token-level labels. This opens up new possibilities, as for many tasks currently addressed by human extractors, raw input and output data are available, but not token-level labels.

1 Introduction

Humans spend countless hours extracting structured machine readable information from unstructured information in a multitude of domains. Promising to automate this, information extraction (IE) is one of the most sought-after industrial applications of natural language processing. However, despite substantial research efforts, in practice, many applications still rely on manual effort to extract the relevant information.

One of the main bottlenecks is a shortage of the data required to train state-of-the-art IE models, which rely on sequence tagging (Finkel et al., 2005; Zhai et al., 2017). Such models require sufficient amounts of training data that is labeled at the token-level, i.e., with one label for each word.

The reason token-level labels are in short supply is that they are not the intended output of human IE tasks. Creating token-level labels thus requires an additional effort, essentially doubling the work required to process each item. This additional effort is expensive and infeasible for many production systems: estimates put the average cost for a sentence at about 3 dollars, and about half an hour annotator time (Alonso et al., 2016). Consequently, state-of-the-art IE approaches, relying on sequence taggers, cannot be applied to many real life IE tasks.

What is readily available in abundance and at no additional costs, is the raw, unstructured input and machine-readable output to a human IE task. Consider the transcription of receipts, checks, or business documents, where the input is an unstructured PDF and the output a row in a database (due date, payable amount, etc). Another example is flight bookings, where the input is a natural language request from the user, and the output a HTTP request, sent to the airline booking API.

To better exploit such existing data sources, we propose an end-to-end (E2E) model based on pointer networks with attention, which can be trained end-to-end on the input/output pairs of human IE tasks, without requiring token-level annotations.

We evaluate our model on three traditional IE data sets. Note that our model and the baselines are competing in two dimensions. The first is cost and applicability. The baselines require token-level labels, which are expensive and unavailable for many real life tasks. Our model does *not* re-

Proceedings of the First Workshop on Speech-Centric Natural Language Processing, pages 48–52
Copenhagen, Denmark, September 7–11, 2017. ©2017 Association for Computational Linguistics

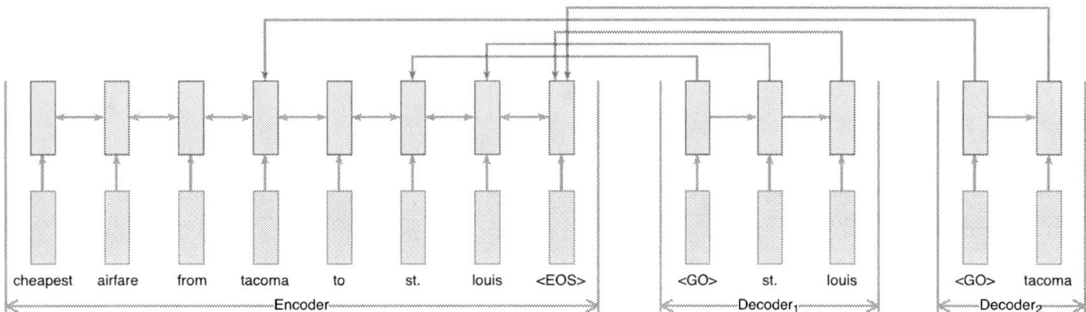

Figure 1: Our model based on pointer networks. The solid red lines are the attention weights. For clarity only two decoders are drawn and only the strongest attention weight for each output is drawn.

quire such token-level labels. Given the time and money required for these annotations, our model clearly improves over the baselines in this dimension. The second dimension is the accuracy of the models. Here we show that our model is competitive with the baseline models on two of the data sets and only slightly worse on the last data set, all despite fewer available annotations.

Contributions We present an E2E IE model with attention that does not depend on costly token-level labels, yet performs competitively with neural baseline models that rely on token-level labels. By saving both time and money at comparable performance, our model presents a viable alternative for many real-life IE needs. Code is available at github.com/rasmusbergpalm/e2e-ie-release

2 Model

Our proposed model is based on pointer networks (Vinyals et al., 2015). A pointer network is a sequence-to-sequence model with attention in which the output is a position in the input sequence. The input position is "pointed to" using the attention mechanism. See figure 1 for an overview. Our formulation of the pointer network is slightly different from the original: Our output is some content from the input rather than a position in the input.

An input sequence of N words $\mathbf{x} = x_1, ..., x_N$ is encoded into another sequence of length N using an Encoder.

$$e_i = \text{Encoder}(x_i, e_{i-1}) \qquad (1)$$

We use a single shared encoder, and $k = 1..K$ decoders, one for each piece of information we wish

to extract. At each step j each decoder calculate an unnormalized scalar attention score a_{kji} over each input position i. The k'th decoder output at step j, o_{kj}, is then the weighted sum of inputs, weighted with the normalized attention scores att_{kji}.

$$d_{kj} = \text{Decoder}_k(o_{k,j-1}, d_{k,j-1}) \qquad (2)$$
$$a_{kji} = \text{Attention}_k(d_{kj}, e_i) \text{ for } i = 1..N \qquad (3)$$
$$att_{kji} = \text{softmax}(a_{kji}) \text{ for } i = 1..N \qquad (4)$$
$$o_{kj} = \sum_{i=1}^{N} att_{kji}\, x_i . \qquad (5)$$

Since each x_i is a one-hot encoded word, and the att_{kji} sum to one over i, o_{kj} is a probability distribution over words.

The loss function is the sum of the negative cross entropy for each of the expected outputs y_{kj} and decoder outputs o_{kj}.

$$\mathcal{L}(\mathbf{x}, \mathbf{y}) = -\sum_{k=1}^{K} \frac{1}{M_k} \sum_{j=1}^{M_k} y_{kj} \log\left(o_{kj}\right) , \qquad (6)$$

where M_k is the sequence length of expected output y_k.

The specific architecture depends on the choice of Encoder, Decoder and Attention. For the encoder, we use a Bi-LSTM with 128 hidden units and a word embedding of 96 dimensions. We use a separate decoder for each of the fields. Each decoder has a word embedding of 96 dimensions, a LSTM with 128 units, with a learned first hidden state and its own attention mechanism. Our attention mechanism follows Bahdanau et al. (2014)

$$a_{ji} = v^T \tanh(W_e\, enc_i + W_d\, dec_j) . \qquad (7)$$

49

The attention parameters W_e, W_d and v for each attention mechanism are all 128-dimensional.

During training we use teacher forcing for the decoders (Williams and Zipser, 1989), such that $o_{k,j-1} = y_{k,j-1}$. During testing we use argmax to select the most probable output for each step j and run each decoder until the first end of sentence (EOS) symbol.

3 Experiments

3.1 Data sets

To compare our model to baselines relying on token-level labels we use existing data sets for which token level-labels are available. We measure our performance on the ATIS data set (Price, 1990) (4978 training samples, 893 testing samples) and the MIT restaurant (7660 train, 1521 test) and movie corpus (9775 train, 2443 test) (Liu et al., 2013). These data sets contains token-level labels in the Beginning-Inside-Out format (BIO).

The ATIS data set consists of natural language requests to a simulated airline booking system. Each word is labeled with one of several classes, e.g. departure city, arrival city, cost, etc. The MIT restaurant and movie corpus are similar, except for a restaurant and movie domain respectively. See table 1 for samples.

MIT Restaurant		MIT Movie	
2	`B-Rating`	show	`O`
start	`I-Rating`	me	`O`
restaurants	`O`	films	`O`
with	`O`	elvis	`B-ACTOR`
inside	`B-Amenity`	films	`O`
dining	`I-Amenity`	set	`B-PLOT`
		in	`I-PLOT`
		hawaii	`I-PLOT`

Table 1: Samples from the MIT restaurant and movie corpus. The transcription errors are part of the data.

Since our model does not need token-level labels, we create an E2E version of each data set without token-level labels by chunking the BIO-labeled words and using the labels as fields to extract. If there are multiple outputs for a single field, e.g. multiple destination cities, we join them with a comma. For the ATIS data set, we choose the 10 most common labels, and we use all the labels for the movie and restaurant corpus. The movie data set has 12 fields and the restaurant has

8. See Table 2 for an example of the E2E ATIS data set.

Input
cheapest airfare from tacoma to st. louis and detroit

Output	
`fromloc`	tacoma
`toloc`	st. louis , detroit
`airline_name`	-
`cost_relative`	cheapest
`period_of_day`	-
`time`	-
`time_relative`	-
`day_name`	-
`day_number`	-
`month_name`	-

Table 2: Sample from the E2E ATIS data set.

3.2 Baselines

For the baselines, we use a two layer neural network model. The first layer is a Bi-directional Long Short Term Memory network (Hochreiter and Schmidhuber, 1997) (Bi-LSTM) and the second layer is a forward-only LSTM. Both layers have 128 hidden units. We use a trained word embedding of size 128. The baseline is trained with Adam (Kingma and Ba, 2014) on the BIO labels and uses early stopping on a held out validation set.

This baseline architecture achieves a fairly strong F1 score of 0.9456 on the ATIS data set. For comparison, the published state-of-the-art is at 0.9586 (Zhai et al., 2017). These numbers are for the traditional BIO token level measure of performance using the publicly available conlleval script. They should not be confused with the E2E performance reported later. We present them here so that readers familiar with the ATIS data set can evaluate the strength of our baselines using a well-known measure.

For the E2E performance measure we train the baseline models using token-level BIO labels and predict BIO labels on the test set. Given the predicted BIO labels, we create the E2E output for the baseline models in the same way we created the E2E data sets, i.e. by chunking and extracting labels as fields. We evaluate our model and the baselines using the MUC-5 definitions of precision, recall and F1, without partial matches (Chinchor and

Sundheim, 1993). We use bootstrap sampling to estimate the probability that the model with the best micro average F1 score on the entire test set is worse for a randomly sampled subset of the test data.

3.3 Our model

Since our decoders can only output values that are present in the input, we prepend a single comma to every input sequence. We optimize our model using Adam and use early stopping on a held-out validation set. The model quickly converges to optimal performance, usually after around 5000 updates after which it starts overfitting.

For the restaurant data set, to increase performance, we double the sizes of all the parameters and use embedding and recurrent dropout following (Gal, 2015). Further, we add a summarizer LSTM to each decoder. The summarizer LSTM reads the entire encoded input. The last hidden state of the summarizer LSTM is then concatenated to each input to the decoder.

3.4 Results

Data set	Baseline	Ours	p
ATIS	0.977	0.974	0.1755
Movie	0.816	0.817	0.3792
Restaurant	**0.724**	0.694	0.0001

Table 3: Micro average F1 scores on the E2E data sets. Results that are significantly better ($p < 0.05$) are highlighted in bold.

We see in Table 3 that our model is competitive with the baseline models in terms of micro-averaged F1 for two of the three data sets. This is a remarkable result given that the baselines are trained on token-level labels, whereas our model is trained end-to-end. For the restaurant data set, our model is slightly worse than the baseline.

4 Related work

Event extraction (EE) is similar to the E2E IE task we propose, except that it can have several event types and multiple events per input. In our E2E IE task, we only have a single event type and assume there is zero or one event mentioned in the input, which is an easier task. Recently, Nguyen et al. (2016) achieved state of the art results on the ACE 2005 EE data set using a recurrent neural network to jointly model event triggers and argument roles.

Other approaches have addressed the need for token-level labels when only raw output values are available. Mintz et al. (2009) introduced distant supervision, which heuristically generates the token-level labels from the output values. You do this by searching for input tokens that matches output values. The matching tokens are then assigned the labels for the matching outputs. One drawback is that the quality of the labels crucially depend on the search algorithm and how closely the tokens match the output values, which makes it brittle. Our method is trained end-to-end, thus not relying on brittle heuristics.

Sutskever et al. (2014) opened up the sequence-to-sequence paradigm. With the addition of attention (Bahdanau et al., 2014), these models achieved state-of-the-art results in machine translation (Wu et al., 2016). We are broadly inspired by these results to investigate E2E models for IE.

The idea of copying words from the input to the output have been used in machine translation to overcome problems with out-of-vocabulary words (Gulcehre et al., 2016; Gu et al., 2016).

5 Discussion

We present an end-to-end IE model that does not require detailed token-level labels. Despite being trained end-to-end, it is competitive with baseline models relying on token-level labels. In contrast to them, our model can be used on many real life IE tasks where intermediate token-level labels are not available and creating them is not feasible.

In our experiments our model and the baselines had access to the same amount of training samples. In a real life scenario it is likely that token-level labels only exist for a subset of all the data. It would be interesting to investigate the quantity/quality trade-of of the labels, and a multi task extension to the model, which could make use of available token-level labels.

Our model is remarkably stable to hyper parameter changes. On the restaurant dataset we tried several different architectures and hyper parameters before settling on the reported one. The difference between the worst and the best was approximately 2 percentage points.

A major limitation of the proposed model is that it can only output values that are present in the input. This is a problem for outputs that are normalized before being submitted as machine readable data, which is a common occurrence. For instance, dates might appear as 'Jan 17 2012' in the input and as '17-01-2012' in the machine readable output.

While it is clear that this model does not solve all the problems present in real-life IE tasks, we believe it is an important step towards applicable E2E IE systems.

In the future, we will experiment with adding character level models on top of the pointer network outputs so the model can focus on an input, and then normalize it to fit the normalized outputs.

Acknowledgments

We would like to thank the reviewers who helped make the paper more concise. Dirk Hovy was supported by the Eurostars grant E10138 ReProsis. This research was supported by the NVIDIA Corporation with the donation of TITAN X GPUs.

References

Héctor Martínez Alonso, Djamé Seddah, and Benoît Sagot. 2016. From Noisy Questions to Minecraft Texts: Annotation Challenges in Extreme Syntax Scenarios. *WNUT 2016* page 13.

Dzmitry Bahdanau, Kyunghyun Cho, and Yoshua Bengio. 2014. Neural machine translation by jointly learning to align and translate. *arXiv preprint arXiv:1409.0473* .

Nancy Chinchor and Beth Sundheim. 1993. MUC-5 Evaluation Metrics. In *Proceedings of the 5th Conference on Message Understanding*. Association for Computational Linguistics, MUC5 '93, pages 69–78. https://doi.org/10.3115/1072017.1072026.

Jenny Rose Finkel, Trond Grenager, and Christopher Manning. 2005. Incorporating Non-local Information into Information Extraction Systems by Gibbs Sampling. In *Proceedings of the 43rd Annual Meeting on Association for Computational Linguistics*. Association for Computational Linguistics, Stroudsburg, PA, USA, ACL '05, pages 363–370.

Yarin Gal. 2015. A Theoretically Grounded Application of Dropout in Recurrent Neural Networks. *arXiv:1512.05287 [stat]* ArXiv: 1512.05287. http://arxiv.org/abs/1512.05287.

Jiatao Gu, Zhengdong Lu, Hang Li, and Victor OK Li. 2016. Incorporating copying mechanism in sequence-to-sequence learning. *arXiv preprint arXiv:1603.06393* .

Caglar Gulcehre, Sungjin Ahn, Ramesh Nallapati, Bowen Zhou, and Yoshua Bengio. 2016. Pointing the unknown words. *arXiv preprint arXiv:1603.08148* .

Sepp Hochreiter and Jürgen Schmidhuber. 1997. Long Short-Term Memory. *Neural Comput.* 9(8):1735–1780. https://doi.org/10.1162/neco.1997.9.8.1735.

Diederik Kingma and Jimmy Ba. 2014. Adam: A Method for Stochastic Optimization. *arXiv:1412.6980 [cs]* ArXiv: 1412.6980. http://arxiv.org/abs/1412.6980.

Jingjing Liu, Panupong Pasupat, Scott Cyphers, and Jim Glass. 2013. Asgard: A portable architecture for multilingual dialogue systems. In *Acoustics, Speech and Signal Processing (ICASSP), 2013 IEEE International Conference on*. IEEE, pages 8386–8390.

Mike Mintz, Steven Bills, Rion Snow, and Dan Jurafsky. 2009. Distant supervision for relation extraction without labeled data. In *Proceedings of the Joint Conference of the 47th Annual Meeting of the ACL and the 4th International Joint Conference on Natural Language Processing of the AFNLP: Volume 2-Volume 2*. Association for Computational Linguistics, pages 1003–1011.

Thien Huu Nguyen, Kyunghyun Cho, and Ralph Grishman. 2016. Joint event extraction via recurrent neural networks. In *Proceedings of NAACL-HLT*. pages 300–309.

Patti Price. 1990. Evaluation of spoken language systems: The ATIS domain. In *Proceedings of the Third DARPA Speech and Natural Language Workshop*. Morgan Kaufmann, pages 91–95.

Ilya Sutskever, Oriol Vinyals, and Quoc V Le. 2014. Sequence to sequence learning with neural networks. In *Advances in neural information processing systems*. pages 3104–3112.

Oriol Vinyals, Meire Fortunato, and Navdeep Jaitly. 2015. Pointer networks. In *Advances in Neural Information Processing Systems*. pages 2692–2700.

Ronald J Williams and David Zipser. 1989. A learning algorithm for continually running fully recurrent neural networks. *Neural computation* 1(2):270–280.

Yonghui Wu, Mike Schuster, Zhifeng Chen, Quoc V Le, Mohammad Norouzi, Wolfgang Macherey, Maxim Krikun, Yuan Cao, Qin Gao, Klaus Macherey, and others. 2016. Google's Neural Machine Translation System: Bridging the Gap between Human and Machine Translation. *arXiv preprint arXiv:1609.08144* .

Feifei Zhai, Saloni Potdar, Bing Xiang, and Bowen Zhou. 2017. Neural Models for Sequence Chunking. *arXiv preprint arXiv:1701.04027* .

Spoken Term Discovery for Language Documentation using Translations

Antonios Anastasopoulos[♠*] Sameer Bansal[◇*]
Sharon Goldwater[◇] Adam Lopez[◇] David Chiang[♠]
[♠]Department of Computer Science and Engineering, University of Notre Dame
[◇]School of Informatics, University of Edinburgh

Abstract

Vast amounts of speech data collected for language documentation and research remain untranscribed and unsearchable, but often a small amount of speech may have text translations available. We present a method for partially labeling additional speech with translations in this scenario. We modify an unsupervised speech-to-translation alignment model and obtain prototype speech segments that match the translation words, which are in turn used to discover terms in the unlabelled data. We evaluate our method on a Spanish-English speech translation corpus and on two corpora of endangered languages, Arapaho and Ainu, demonstrating its appropriateness and applicability in an actual very-low-resource scenario.

1 Introduction

Language documentation efforts over the last 50–60 years have resulted in audio recordings of native speakers in a large number of languages, many of which are available online. However, due to the enormous effort required for transcription, much of the data remains unannotated and unsearchable.[1] For example, out of the 137 unrestricted collections in the Archive of the Indigenous Languages of Latin America, about half (49%) contain no transcriptions at all, and only 7% are fully transcribed.[2] As a result, some recent documentation efforts have begun to focus instead on annotating with *translations*, often with the help of bilingual

native speakers themsclvcs (Bird et al., 2014; Blachon et al., 2016; Adda et al., 2016).

Nevertheless, even translation takes time and language knowledge, so there may still be little translated data relative to the amount of recorded audio. An important goal, then, is to bootstrap language technology from this small parallel corpus in order to provide tools to annotate more data or make the data more searchable.

We build on the approach of Anastasopoulos et al. (2016), who developed a system that performs joint inference to identify recurring segments of audio and cluster them while aligning them to words in a text translation. Here, we extend the method to be able to search for new instances of the latent clusters within the unlabeled audio, effectively providing keyword translations for some of the unlabeled speech. We evaluate our method on a Spanish-English corpus used in previous work, and on two datasets from endangered languages (narratives in Arapaho and Ainu). No previous computational methods have been tested on the latter data, to our knowledge. We show that in all cases, our system outperforms a recent baseline targeted at the same very low-resource setting (Bansal et al., 2017b), also showing robustness to audio quality and preprocessing decisions.

2 Related work

Our work joins a handful of other recent proposals aimed at low-resource speech-to-text alignment and translation. These include those of Duong et al. (2016) and Anastasopoulos et al. (2016), who performed alignment only; Bérard et al. (2016), who used synthetic rather than real speech; and Adams et al. (2016) and Godard et al. (2016), who worked from phone lattices and phone sequences, respectively; Stahlberg et al. (2013), who perform phone-to-translation alignment for pronunci-

---

* Equal contribution.

[1]By some estimates, a trained linguist requires up to one hour for to phonetically transcribe one minute of speech (Thi-Ngoc-Diep Do and Castelli, 2014).

[2]http://ailla.utexas.org

53

Proceedings of the First Workshop on Speech-Centric Natural Language Processing, pages 53–58
Copenhagen, Denmark, September 7–11, 2017. ©2017 Association for Computational Linguistics

ation extraction. Weiss et al. (2017) presented a sequence-to-sequence neural model that learned a direct mapping from speech to translated text with impressive results, but was trained on roughly 140 hours of parallel data—far more than is available for most endangered languages.

The only previous system we know of to address the same very-low-resource scenario and provide translation terms for unlabeled audio is that of Bansal et al. (2017b) (henceforth UTD-align), who used an unsupervised term discovery system (Jansen et al., 2010) to cluster recurring audio segments into pseudowords. The pseudowords occurring in the parallel section of the corpus were then aligned to the translation text using IBM Model 1, and used to translate instances occurring in the test (audio-only) section.

3   Method

The main difference between our method and UTD-align is that UTD-align clusters the audio prior to aligning with the translations, whereas we start by performing joint alignment and clustering using an improved version of the method proposed by Anastasopoulos et al. (2016) (henceforth s2t). The resulting aligned clusters are represented by one or more prototype speech segments. We extend s2t to identify new instances of those prototypes in the unlabeled speech, using a modified version of ZRTools, the same UTD toolkit used by UTD-align.[3] (Jansen et al., 2010)

Previous work has indicated that using translation text to inform acoustic clustering provides more accurate clusters than just using UTD (Bansal et al., 2017a), so we initially expected that this straightforward extension of s2t would work better than UTD-align. However, early experiments indicated that the text had *too* much influence on clustering, yielding clusters with highly diverse audio, and thus poor prototypes. Thus, we modified s2t[4] in order to account for this issue, obtaining prototypes of higher quality (§3.1), which we search for in the unlabeled audio (§3.2).

3.1   Aligning speech to translation

The s2t model is an extension of IBM Model 2 for word alignment (Brown et al., 1993), combined with K-means clustering using Dynamic Time Warping (DTW) (Berndt and Clifford,

1994) as a distance measure. It uses expectation-maximization (EM) to align speech segments to words in the parallel text, while jointly clustering the segments. Each translation word is aligned to an acoustic segment, with overlapping alignments and unaligned speech spans being allowed.

In the original implementation, every translation word was represented by a fixed number (2) of acoustic sub-clusters, with a single prototype representing each.[5] The prototypes are averages of the segments in the cluster, computed using DTW Barycenter Averaging (Petitjean et al., 2011). At the E-step, each segment was assigned to its closest sub-cluster, and at the M-step the sub-cluster's prototype was re-computed. However, the original choice of two subclusters was fairly arbitrary, and we found it doesn't sufficiently account for the wide acoustic variability due to gender or speaker. We thus modify s2t so that, before the M-step, each cluster's segments are grouped into sub-clusters using connected components clustering with a similarity threshold δ, following Park and Glass (2008). That way, the number of sub-clusters and prototypes for each translation word is determined automatically based on the acoustic similarity of the segments.

Our preliminary analysis showed that shorter alignments tend to introduce significantly more noise than longer ones. Therefore, in the final M-step of s2t, we discard all segments shorter than a length threshold t before computing the prototypes. We use the default values for the rest of the s2t parameters.

Another pragmatic choice we made based on the performance of our method was to remove the stopwords from the translations, following Bansal et al. (2017b). The rationale is that translation stopwords would not be particularly useful for labelling speech in our envisioned use cases.

3.2   Keyword Search

In the second stage, we use the approximate DTW-based pattern matching method of ZRTools to search for the obtained prototypes in the test data. We require that each discovered term matches at least $k\%$ of a prototype's length and that its DTW similarity score is higher than a threshold s. By varying s we can control the number of discovered terms, trading off precision and recall. Also, we do not allow overlapping matches; in the case

---

[3] https://github.com/arenjansen/ZRTools
[4] The code is available at https://bitbucket.org/ndnlp/translationTermDiscovery

[5] https://bitbucket.org/ndnlp/speech2translation

of an overlap, we output the match with the higher score.

4 Experiments

The CALLHOME Spanish Speech dataset (LDC2014T23) with English translations (Post et al., 2013) has been used in almost all ground-laying previous work, treating Spanish as a low-resource language. As a collection of telephone conversations between relatives (about 20 total hours of audio), it doesn't match our language documentation scenario, but we use it in order to compare our method with previous work.

We shuffle the utterances and split them into training, dev, and test sets with 70%, 10%, and 20% of the data, respectively. We filter the active audio regions using energy-based voice activity detection (VAD). We obtain prototypes in the training set and tune the values of the length threshold t, the similarity threshold d, and the partial overlap threshold k on the development set using grid search. The best parameter combination is t = 300 ms, d = 90%, and k = 80%, while s = 0.90 returns the highest F-score. We evaluate our discovered translation terms on the test set using precision, recall, and F-score at the token level over the correct bag-of-words translations.

We also evaluate our method on two low-resource endangered languages, Arapaho and Ainu. For these experiments, we only have a training and test set, so we use the same preprocessing and hyperparameter settings as in CALLHOME.

Arapaho is an Algonquian language with about 1,000 native speakers, mostly in Wyoming. We use 8 narratives published at The Arapaho Language Project,[6] which provides the narratives' audio along with English translations, among other language learning resources.

Hokkaido Ainu is the sole surviving member of the Ainu language family and is generally considered a language isolate. As of 2007, only ten native speakers were alive. The Glossed Audio Corpus of Ainu Folklore provides 10 narratives with audio and translations in English.[7] More information and statistics on the Arapaho and Ainu corpora is provided in Tables 4 and 5.

Method	Prec	Rec	F-score	Coverage
UTD-align	5.1	2.1	3.0	27%
ours	4.2	3.5	3.8	59%
ours (oracle)	5.3	4.9	5.1	65%

Table 1: Results of our method and baseline work on the CALLHOME dataset. Our method improves over UTD-align whether inferring alignments or using oracle (silver) alignments.

4.1 Results on CALLHOME

We first evaluate the effect of our modifications to the s2t method, by calculating alignment F-score on links between speech frames and translation words.[8] The intermediate sub-clustering step between the E- and M-steps results in a more informed selection of the number of sub-clusters that increases the alignment F-score by 1.5%. Also, removing translation stopwords further leads to higher alignment precision by +4%. Alignment recall is lower since it's computed over the alignments of both content and stopwords. Although both improvements are small, the higher alignment precision leads to better prototypes.

In addition, Duong et al. (2016) created "silver" standard speech-to-translation alignments by combining the forced speech-to-transcription alignments and the transcription-to-translation word alignments. These are useful for evaluating how well the prototype creation and matching could work, given oracle speech-to-translation alignments. In Table 1, we report precision, recall, and F-score on the discovered translation terms (at the token level) using prototypes from both "silver" and noisy alignments. We also report the percentage of active audio that is labelled (coverage). In both cases we outperform UTD-align.[9] Even though there is room for improvement, using the translation information at the alignment stage certainly improves the clustering, as anticipated. Another advantage of our method over UTD-align is its significantly improved coverage of the active audio, as shown in the last column of Table 1. The precision-recall curve obtained by varying the output similarity threshold s is shown in Figure 1.

---

[6]http://www.colorado.edu/csilw/alp/index.html
[7]http://ainucorpus.ninjal.ac.jp/corpus/en/

[8]See the paper by Duong et al. (2016) for a full definition.
[9]The code was provided by the authors of UTD-align.

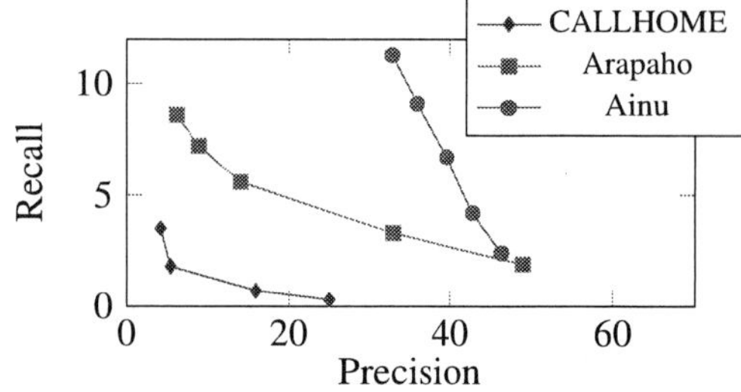

Figure 1: Average precision and recall curve for our discovered matches in CALLHOME and the Arapaho and Ainu test narratives (varying the output threshold s between 0.90 and 0.94).

Arapaho narrative	Terms found	Prec (%)	Rec (%)	Oracle Recall
1	29	31.0	4.7	32.3
2	65	21.5	8.0	44.3
3	91	7.7	6.4	54.5
4	158	13.9	8.4	53.4
6	1	100.0	0.7	41.4
7	104	7.7	7.1	44.6
8	10	30.0	4.5	65.2
average-ours	65	14.0	6.0	
UTD-align	2	26.7	0.4	

Table 2: Results on Arapaho narratives. In general, we identify meaningful translation terms.

4.2 Results on Arapaho and Ainu

Out of the eight Arapaho narratives, we select the longest (18 minutes of audio, 233 English word types) for training, using the other seven (32 minutes total) for evaluation. The Ainu collection provides ten narratives, so we use the first two for training (24 minutes of audio, 494 English word types) and the rest (133 minutes total) as test data.

Treating each narrative as a bag of words, the precision and recall results at the token level are shown in Tables 2 and 3. The last columns of these Tables correspond to the highest possible recall that we could get if we discovered all the training terms that also appear in the test set. Precision-recall curves can be seen in Figure 1.

On both corpora, UTD-align identifies hardly any translation terms, with recall scores below 1% and average F-scores of 0.8% and 0.2% for Arapaho and Ainu, respectively. Preprocessing with the same VAD script as for our method, UTD-align produced too many spurious matches

Ainu narrative	Terms found	Prec (%)	Rec (%)	Oracle Recall
3	80	50.0	3.8	63.0
4	73	49.3	4.5	67.1
5	199	49.7	5.1	61.8
6	174	22.4	9.0	65.0
7	123	19.5	8.9	56.1
8	122	57.4	3.9	67.8
9	59	62.7	1.5	63.0
10	149	46.3	6.6	69.7
average-ours	122	42.3	4.2	
UTD-align	4	24.2	0.1	

Table 3: Results on the Ainu narratives. We are able to correctly identify several terms per story, with quite high precision.

(millions); we then used a more aggressive filtering which removed more parts of the audio, but it resulted in too few discovered matches (as shown here). In principle, it should be possible to tailor the preprocessing parameters for each corpus and improve results for UTD-align.

Our method, instead, outputs several terms per narrative without the need to readjust preprocessing decisions, with F-scores of 8.4% (Arapaho) and 7.2% (Ainu). Two exceptions are Arapaho narratives #6 and #8, which, unlike our training data, are narrated by a woman. Although there is clearly room for improvement in terms of recall, as shown by the last columns of Tables 2 and 3, we are generally able to identify meaningful terms.

For most of the Arapaho stories we discover named entities such as *Ghost* and *Strong Bear*, content nouns like *tipis* and *mountains*, or verbs such as *hunting*. In Ainu we discover more terms, but the narratives are also longer. A larger domain shift between training and test (small overlap on named entities and other content words) leads to lower recall compared to Arapaho. Our method correctly identifies mostly common terms in the Ainu narratives, like *village*, *food*, as well as verbs used in narration such as *said*, *went*, or *came*.

5 Conclusion

We propose a method that modifies and extends a speech-to-translation alignment method and can be used for identifying translation terms in unlabeled audio, appropriate for extremely small datasets. On CALLHOME, we show small improvements over a recent baseline. We also demonstrate the applicability of our method on language documentation scenarios, by applying it on two endangered language datasets. Speaker differences are still an issue, but our method is more robust to differences in acoustic quality than the previous method.

Acknowledgements We are grateful for support from NSF Award 1464553. This work was also supported in part by a James S McDonnell Foundation Scholar Award and a Google faculty research award. Goldwater is the recipient of James S. McDonnell Foundation Scholar Award #220020374.

References

Oliver Adams, Graham Neubig, Trevor Cohn, Steven Bird, Quoc Truong Do, and Satoshi Nakamura. 2016. Learning a lexicon and translation model from phoneme lattices. In *Proc. EMNLP*, pages 2377–2382.

Gilles Adda, Sebastian Stüker, Martine Adda-Decker, Odette Ambouroue, Laurent Besacier, David Blachon, Hélène Bonneau-Maynard, Pierre Godard, Fatima Hamlaoui, Dmitry Idiatov, et al. 2016. Breaking the unwritten language barrier: The BULB project. *Procedia Computer Science*, 81:8–14.

Antonios Anastasopoulos, David Chiang, and Long Duong. 2016. An unsupervised probability model for speech-to-translation alignment of low-resource languages. In *Proc. EMNLP*, pages 1255–1263.

Sameer Bansal, Herman Kamper, Sharon Goldwater, and Adam Lopez. 2017a. Weakly supervised spoken term discovery using cross-lingual side information. In *Proc. ICASSP*.

Sameer Bansal, Herman Kamper, Adam Lopez, and Sharon Goldwater. 2017b. Towards speech-to-text translation without speech recognition. In *Proc. EACL, Vol. 2*, pages 474–479.

Alexandre Bérard, Olivier Pietquin, Christophe Servan, and Laurent Besacier. 2016. Listen and translate: A proof of concept for end-to-end speech-to-text translation. In *Proc. NIPS End-to-end Learning for Speech and Audio Processing Workshop*.

Donald J. Berndt and James Clifford. 1994. Using dynamic time warping to find patterns in time series. In *Proc. KDD*, pages 359–370.

Steven Bird, Lauren Gawne, Katie Gelbart, and Isaac McAlister. 2014. Collecting bilingual audio in remote indigenous communities. In *Proc. COLING*, pages 1015–1024.

David Blachon, Elodie Gauthier, Laurent Besacier, Guy-Noël Kouarata, Martine Adda-Decker, and Annie Rialland. 2016. Parallel speech collection for under-resourced language studies using the Lig-Aikuma mobile device app. *Procedia Computer Science*, 81:61–66.

Peter F. Brown, Vincent J. Della Pietra, Stephen A. Della Pietra, and Robert L. Mercer. 1993. The mathematics of statistical machine translation: Parameter estimation. *Computational Linguistics*, 19(2):263–311.

Long Duong, Antonios Anastasopoulos, David Chiang, Steven Bird, and Trevor Cohn. 2016. An attentional model for speech translation without transcription. In *Proc. NAACL-HLT*, pages 949–959.

Pierre Godard, Gilles Adda, Martine Adda-Decker, Alexandre Allauzen, Laurent Besacier, Helene Bonneau-Maynard, Guy-Noël Kouarata, Kevin Löser, Annie Rialland, and François Yvon. 2016. Preliminary experiments on unsupervised word discovery in Mboshi. In *Proc. INTERSPEECH*.

Aren Jansen, Kenneth Church, and Hynek Hermansky. 2010. Towards spoken term discovery at scale with zero resources. In *Proc. INTERSPEECH*, pages 1676–1679.

Alex S. Park and James R. Glass. 2008. Unsupervised pattern discovery in speech. *IEEE Trans. Audio, Speech, and Language Processing*, 16(1):186–197.

François Petitjean, Alain Ketterlin, and Pierre Gançarski. 2011. A global averaging method for dynamic time warping, with applications to clustering. *Pattern Recognition*, 44(3):678–693.

Matt Post, Gaurav Kumar, Adam Lopez, Damianos Karakos, Chris Callison-Burch, and Sanjeev Khudanpur. 2013. Improved speech-to-text translation with the fisher and callhome spanish-english speech translation corpus. In *Proc. IWSLT*.

Felix Stahlberg, Tim Schlippe, Stephan Vogel, and Tanja Schultz. 2013. Pronunciation extraction from phoneme sequences through cross-lingual word-to-phoneme alignment. In *ICSLSP*, pages 260–272. Springer.

Alexis Michaud Thi-Ngoc-Diep Do and Eric Castelli. 2014. Towards the automatic processing of Yongning Na (Sino-Tibetan): developing a 'light' acoustic model of the target language and testing 'heavyweight' models from five national languages. In *Proc. SLTU*, pages 153–160.

Ron J. Weiss, Jan Chorowski, Navdeep Jaitly, Yonghui Wu, and Zhifeng Chen. 2017. Sequence-to-sequence models can directly transcribe foreign speech. arXiv:1703.08581.

ID	Title	Duration (m:s)	Transcription Tokens	Transcription Types	Translation Tokens	Translation Types
1	Fooling the ghost	5:12	134	91	192	80
2	The Ghost by the Road	7:00	140	104	176	117
3	The Old Couple and the Ghost	3:12	88	71	110	74
4	The Owl Man	7:14	269	157	262	125
5	Strong Bear and the Ghost	18:35	523	346	591	289
6	The Woman who turned into Stone	3:26	140	93	152	85
7	Strong Bear and the Boxer	3:29	125	82	112	61
8	Telescope	1:40	54	48	66	48
	total	50:00	1473	849	1661	556

Table 4: Statistics on the Arapaho narratives. English type and token counts do not include stopwords.

ID	Title	Duration (m:s)	Transcription Types	Transcription Tokens	Translation Types	Translation Tokens
1	Pananpe escapes from the demons hands	6:12	189	849	203	519
2	The Girl who Gave the Bad Red Dog Poison	17:48	488	2634	537	1336
3	The Young Lad Raised by the Cat God	15:14	450	2149	437	1066
4	The Poor Man who Dug Up the Village Chief Wife's Grave	10:38	306	1551	365	796
5	The Grapevines which Warded Off the Topattumi-night Raiders	24:41	572	3600	660	1942
6	The Woman who Became Kemkacikappo Bird	8:59	233	699	219	431
7	The Goddess of the Fire Fought with the Demon God From the End of the Earth	6:03	161	416	156	271
8	The Bridge of Mist	23:09	519	3408	591	1816
9	The Rich Man from Cen-pak	32:59	699	4845	789	2523
10	Godly Elder Sister Gets Rid of Bad Bear Father	12:16	400	1789	401	1043
	total	157:59	1826	21940	1861	11743

Table 5: Statistics on the Ainu narratives. English type and token counts do not include stopwords.

Amharic-English Speech Translation in Tourism Domain

Michael Melese Woldeyohannis
Addis Ababa University, Addis Ababa, Ethiopia
michael.melese@aau.edu.et

Laurent Besacier
LIG Laboratory, UJF, BP53,
38041 Grenoble Cedex 9, France
laurent.besacier@imag.fr

Million Meshesha
Addis Ababa University,
Addis Ababa, Ethiopia
michael.melese@aau.edu.et

Abstract

This paper describes speech translation from Amharic-to-English, particularly Automatic Speech Recognition (ASR) with post-editing feature and Amharic-English Statistical Machine Translation (SMT). ASR experiment is conducted using morpheme language model (LM) and phoneme acoustic model (AM). Likewise, SMT conducted using word and morpheme as unit.

Morpheme based translation shows a 6.29 BLEU score at a 76.4% of recognition accuracy while word based translation shows a 12.83 BLEU score using 77.4% word recognition accuracy. Further, after post-edit on Amharic ASR using corpus based n-gram, the word recognition accuracy increased by 1.42%. Since post-edit approach reduces error propagation, the word based translation accuracy improved by 0.25 (1.95%) BLEU score.

We are now working towards further improving propagated errors through different algorithms at each unit of speech translation cascading component.

1 Introduction

Speech is one of the most natural form of communication for humankind (Honda, 2003). Computer with the ability to understand natural language promoted the development of man-machine interface. This can be extended through different digital platforms such as radio, mobile, TV, CD and others. Through these, speech translation facilitates communication between the people who speak different languages.

Speech translation is the process by which spoken source phrases are translated to a target language using a computer (Gao et al., 2006). Speech translation research for major and technological supported languages like English, European languages (like French and Spanish) and Asian languages (like Japanese and Chinese) has been conducted since the 1983s by NEC Corporation (Kurematsu, 1996). The advancement of speech translation captivates the communication between people who do not share the same language.

The state-of-the-art of speech translation system can be seen as the integration of three major cascading components (Gao et al., 2006; Jurafsky and Martin, 2008); Automatic Speech Recognition (ASR), Machine Translation (MT) and Text-To-Speech (TTS) synthesis.

ASR is the process by which a machine infers spoken words, by means of talking to computer, and having it correctly understand a recorded audio signal. Beside ASR, MT is the process by which a machine is used to translate a text from one source language to another target language. Finally, TTS creates a spoken version from the text of electronic document such as text file and web document.

As one major component of speech translation, Amharic ASR started in 2001 (Melese et al., 2016). A number of attempts have been made for Amharic ASR using different methods and techniques towards designing speaker independent, large vocabulary, contineous speech and spontaneous speech recognition.

In addition to ASR, a preliminary English-Amharic machine translation experiments was conducted using phonemic transcription on the Amharic corpus (Teshome et al., 2015). The result obtained from the experiment shows that, it is possible to design English-Amharic machine translation using statistical method.

As the last component of speech translation, a number of TTS research have been attempted

59

Proceedings of the First Workshop on Speech-Centric Natural Language Processing, pages 59–66
Copenhagen, Denmark, September 7–11, 2017. ©2017 Association for Computational Linguistics

using different techniques and methods as discussed by (Anberbir and Takara, 2009). Among these, concatenative, cepstral, formant and a syllable based speech synthesizers were the main methods and techniques applied.

All the above research works were conducted using different methods and techniques beside data difference and integration as a cascading component. Moreover, dataset and tools used in the above research are not accessible which makes difficult to evaluate the advancement of research in speech technology for local languages.

However, there is no attempt to integrate ASR, SMT and TTS to come up with speech translation system for Amharic language. Thus, the main aim of this study is to investigate the possibility to design Amharic-English speech translation system that controls recognition errors propagating through cascading components.

2 Amharic Language

Amharic is a Semitic language derived from Ge'ez with the second largest speaker in the world next to Arabic (Simons and Fennig, 2017). The name Amharic (አማርኛ) comes from the district of Amhara (አማራ) in northern Ethiopia, which is thought to be the historic, classical and ecclesiastical language of Ethiopia. Moreover, the language Amharic has five dialectical variations spoken named as: Addis Ababa, Gojam, Gonder, Wollo and Menz.

Amharic is the official working language of government of Ethiopia among the 89 languages registered in the country with up to 200 different spoken dialects (Simons and Fennig, 2017; Thompson, 2016). Beside these, Amharic language is being used in governmental administration, public media and national commerce of some regional states of the country. This includes; Addis Ababa, Amhara, Diredawa and Southern Nations, Nationalities and People (SNNP).

Amharic language is spoken by more than 25 million with up to 22 million native speakers. The majority of Amharic speakers found in Ethiopia even though there are also speakers in a number of other countries, particularly Italy, Canada, the USA and Sweden.

Unlike other Semitic languages, such as Arabic and Hebrew, modern Amharic script has inherited its writing system from Ge'ez (ግዕዝ) (Yimam, 2000). Amharic language uses a grapheme based writing system called fidel (ፊደል) written and read from left to right. Amharic graphemes are represented as a sequence of consonant vowel (CV) pairs, the basic shape determined by the consonant, which is modified for the vowel.

The Amharic writing system is composed of four distinct categories consisting of 276 different symbols; 33 core characters with 7 orders (አ, ኡ, ኢ, አ, ኤ, እ and ኦ), 4 labiovelars with 5 orders symbol (ቅ, ጎ, ኅ and ግ), 18 labialized consonants with 1 order (ሟ) and 1 labiodental characters consisting 7 orders (ቨ, ቩ, ቪ, ቫ, ቬ, ቭ and ቮ).

In Amharic writing system, all the 276 distinct orthographic representation are indispensable due to their distinct orthographic representation.

However, as part of speech translation, speech recognition mainly deals with distinct sound. Among those, some of the graphemes generate same sound like (ሀ, ሐ, ኀ and ኸ) pronounced as h/ʊ/.

On the other hand, Machine translation emphasizes on orthographic representation which result the same meaning in different graphemes. As a result, normalization is required to minimize the graphemes variation which leads to better translation while minimizing the ASR model. Table 1 presents the Amharic character set before and after normalization.

	Unnormalized	Normalized	Difference
Core Character	33	27	6
Labiovelar	4	4	0
Labialized	18	18	0
Labiodental	1	1	0
Total	276	234	42

Table 1: Distribution of Amharic character set adopted and modified from (Melese et al., 2016)

As a result, graphemes that generate the same sound are normalized in to the seven order of core character. The normalization is based on the usage of most characters frequency in Amharic text document. This includes, normalization from (ሀ, ሐ, ኀ and ኸ) to ሀ, (ሰ, ሠ) to ሰ, (ጸ, ፀ) to ጸ and (ጸ, ፀ) to ጸ along with order.

3 Tourism in Ethiopia

Tourism is the activity of traveling to and staying in places outside their usual environment for not more than one year to create a direct contact between people and cultures (UNWTO, 2016). Ethiopia has much to offer for international tourists[1] ranging from the peaks of the rugged Semien mountains to the lowest points on earth called Danakil Depression which is more than 400 feet below sea level.

In addition, tourism become a pleasing sustainable economic development that serves as an alternative source of foreign exchange for the counties like Ethiopia.

Moreover, The 2015 United Nations World Tourism report (UNWTO, 2016) and the World Bank[2] report indicate that, in 2015 a total of 864,000 non-resident tourists come to Ethiopia to visit different tourist attraction. These include; ancient, medieval cities and world heritages registered by UNESCO as tourist attraction. Since the year 2010 until 2015, the average number of tourist flow increase by 13.05% per year.

According to Walta Information Center[3], citing Ethiopia Ministry of Culture and Tourism, Ethiopia has secured 872 million dollars in first quarter of its 2016/17 fiscal year from 223,032 international tourists. The revenue was mostly through conference tourism, research business and other activities. Majority of the tourists were from USA, England, Germany, France and Italy speaking foreign languages. Beside this, tourists express their ideas using different languages, the majority of the tourists can speak and communicate in English to exchange information about tourist attractions.

Due to this, language barriers are a major problem for today's global communication (Nakamura, 2009). As a result, they look for an alternate option that lets them communicate with the surrounding.

Thus, speech translation system is one of the best technologies used to fill the communication gap between the people who speak different languages (Nakamura, 2009). This is especially true in overcoming language barriers of today's global communication besides supporting under-resourced language.

However, under-resourced languages such as Amharic, suffer from having a digital text and speech corpus to support speech translation. So, after collecting text and speech corpora, moving

one step further helps in solving language barriers problem.

Therefore, this study attempts to come up with an Amharic-English speech translation system taking tourism as a domain.

4 Data Preparation

Nowadays, Amharic language suffers from a lack of speech and text corpora for ASR and SMT. Beside these, collecting standardized and annotated corpora is one of the most challenging and expensive tasks when working with under resourced languages (Besacier et al., 2006; Gauthier et al., 2016).

For Amharic speech recognition training and development, 20 hours of read speech corpus prepared by Abate et. al (2005) were used. However, due to unavailability of standardized corpora for speech translation in tourism domain, a text corpus is acquired from resourced and technologically supported languages particularly English.

Accordingly, a parallel English-Arabic text data was acquired from the Basic Traveller Expression Corpus (BTEC) 2009 which is made available through International Workshop on Spoken Language Translation (IWSLT) (Kessler, 2010). A parallel Amharic-English corpus has been prepared by translating the English BTEC data using a bilingual speaker. This data is used for the development of speech translation cascading component such as, ASR and SMT.

The corpus has a total of 28,084 Amharic-English parallel sentences. To keep the dataset consistent, the text corpus has been further preprocessed, such as typing errors are corrected, abbreviations have been expanded, numbers have been textually transcribed and concatenated words have been separated.

Amharic speech recognition is conducted using words and morphemes as a language model with a phoneme-based acoustic model. Similarly word and morpheme have been used as a translation unit for Amharic in Amharic-English machine translation. Morpheme-based segmentation of training, development, testing obtained by segmenting word into sub-word unit using corpus-based, language independent and unsupervised segmentation for using morfessor 2.0 (Smit et al., 2014).

Once the Amharic-English BTEC corpus is prepared, it is divided into training, tuning and testing set with a proportion of 69.33% (19472 sen-

---

[1]http://www.investethiopia.gov.et/
images/pdf/Investment_Brochure_to_
Ethiopia.pdf
[2] http://data.worldbank.org/indicator/
ST.INT.ARVL?end=2015
[3]https://www.waltainfo.com/
FeaturedArticles/detail?cid=28751

tences), 1.78%(500 sentences) and 28.88%(8112 sentences), respectively.

Then, the 8112 (28.38%) test set sentences are recorded under a normal office environment from eight (4 Male and 4 Female) native Amharic speakers using LIG-Aikuma, a smartphone based application tool (Blachon et al., 2016).

Accordingly, a total of 7.43 hours read speech corpus ranging from 1,020 ms to 14,633 ms with an average speech time of 3,297 ms has been collected from the tourism domain.

Moreover, as suggested by Melese et al., (2016), morphologically rich and under-resourced language like Amharic provides a better recognition accuracy using morpheme based language model with phoneme based acoustic model.

Similarly, language model data for Amharic speech recognition has been collected from different sources. A text corpus collected for Google project (Tachbelie and Abate, 2015) have been used in addition to BTEC SMT training data excluding the test data. Table 2 presents the training, development and language model data used for Amharic speech recognition.

	Train	Test	Language Model	
			Word	Morpheme
Sentence	10,875	8,112	261,620	261,620
Token	145,404	50,906	4,223,835	5,773,282
Type	24,653	4,035	328,615	141,851

Table 2: Distribution of Amharic data for ASR.

Like speech recognition, a total of 42,134 sentences (374,153 token of 8,678 type) English language model data have been used for Amharic-English machine translation. The data is collected from the same BTEC corpus excluding test data.

Consequently, corpus based and language independent segmentation have been applied on a training, development and test set of Amharic SMT data. Morfessor is used to segment words to a sub word units. Table 3 presents summary of the corpus used for Amharic-English machine translation using word and morpheme as a unit.

Likewise, the post-edit is conducted using a corpus based n-gram approach. Accordingly, a corpus containing 681,910 sentences (11,514,557 tokens) of 582,150 type data crawled from web including news and magazine.

Then, the data is further cleaned, preprocessed and normalized. From this data, a total of 5,057,112 bigram, 8,341,966 trigram, 9,276,600 quadrigram and 9,242,670 pentagram word se-

	Unit		Train	Dev	Test
Amharic	Word	Sentence	19,472	500	8,172
		Token	107,049	2,795	37,288
		Type	18,650	1,470	4,168
	Morpheme	Sentence	19,472	500	8,172
		Token	145,419	3,828	50,906
		Type	15,679	1,621	4,035
English	Word	Sentence	19,472	500	8,172
		Token	157,550	4,024	55,062
		Type	10,544	1,227	3,775

Table 3: Distribution of Amharic-English SMT data.

quences have been extracted after expanding numbers and abbreviation.

5 System Architecture

As discussed in Section 1, the state-of-the-art of speech translation suggest to apply through the integration of cascading components to translate speech from source language (Amharic) to a target language (English).

As part of the cascading components, the output of a speech recognizer contains more and presents a variety of errors. These errors further propagates to the succeeding component of speech translation which results in low performance.

Hence, in this study we propose an Amharic ASR post-editing module that can detect an error, identify possible suggestion and finally correct based on the proposal. The correction is made using n-gram data store using minimum edit disatnce and perplexity before the error heads to statistical machine translation.

Figure 1 presents Amharic-English speech-to-speech translation (S2ST) architecture with and without considering ASR post-edit.

The post-edit process mainly consists of three different phases; error detection, correction proposal and finally suggest correction as depicted in Figure 2.

The first phase of post editing is to detect the error from ASR recognition output. Basically, to detect an error, recognized morpheme units are concatenated to form a word and its existence is checked in unigram Amharic dictionary.

Thus, a morpheme-based speech recognition output "የ+ -ስጦታ እቃ -ተዘነጉ ተስፋ አደር+ -ጋለሁ "[4] concatenated to form a phrase "የስጦታ እቃ -ተዘነጉ ተስፋ አደርጋለሁ ".

---

[4] "+" refers to morphemes followed by other morpheme while "-" refer to leading morpheme is there.

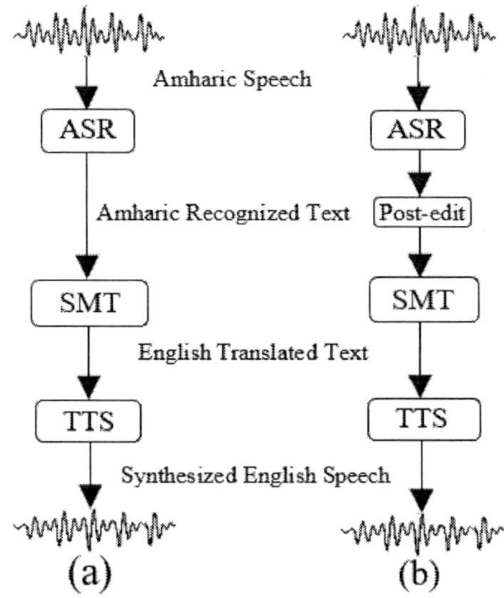

Figure 1: Amharic-English speech-to-speech translation architecture (a) without post-edit (b) with post-edit

If the word is not in the unigram Amharic dictionary, then the "word" is considered as an error and marked as error("*") then it is concatenated to the remaining words. Accordingly, each token checked in unigram dictionary and the word "-ተዘነጉ" is not in dictionary which is marked as an error.

If the error is detected during the first phase, then the correction proposal phase takes the sentence with error mark and creates (w-n+1) n-grams after adding start "<s>" and end "</s>" symbol, where w is number of token in sentence and n specifies n-grams. Otherwise, the sentence is considered as correct.

Consequently, three pantagram word sequences are generated from the speech recognition of "<s> የስጦታ እቃ -ተዘነጉ ተስፋ አደርጋለሁ </s>" sentence. These are;

1. <s> የስጦታ እቃ * ተስፋ

2. የስጦታ እቃ * ተስፋ አደርጋለሁ

3. እቃ * ተስፋ አደርጋለሁ </s>

Subsequently, we select the n-grams with error marks and search in n-gram data store to select possible candidates for correction after removing the error mark. If there is no candidate in n-gram, then go for (n-1)-gram order until bigram.

Once the candidate identified, the suggestion is made taking the minimum edit distance between

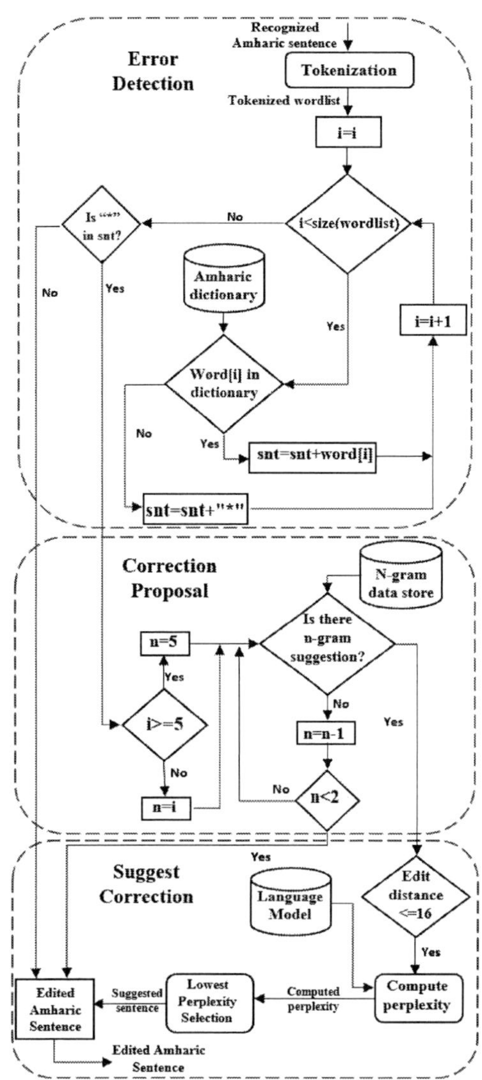

Figure 2: Amharic ASR post-edit algorithm

the error detected and suggestion selected. In this phase, the sum of maximum edit distance has been set experimentally to 16. The maximum edit distance 16 was selected to provide at least one suggestion per sentence and minimize the computation of perplexity. Table 4 depicts a sample of possible correction proposal for a sentence "የስጦታ እቃ -ተዘነጉ ተስፋ አደርጋለሁ".

Finally, the suggestion is made primarily using minimum edit distance then by calculating the perplexity. The minimal edit distance is computed between the word "-ተዘነጉ" and the underlined n-gram based possible suggestion from a sentence of Table 4.

Possible suggestion list	Distance
የስጦታ እቃ ተስፋ አደርጋለሁ ብለዋል	5
የስጦታ እቃ ብየ ተስፋ አደርጋለሁ	5
የስጦታ እቃ አንደማይ ተስፋ አደርጋለሁ	5
የስጦታ እቃ ተስፋ አደርጋለሁ ይላሉ	5
የስጦታ እቃ ተስፋ አደርጋለሁ ለፈገግታ	5
የስጦታ እቃ ብዬ ተስፋ አደርጋለሁ	5
የስጦታ እቃ ተስፋ አደርጋለሁ ብሷል	5
የስጦታ እቃ ተስፋ አደርጋለሁ ይላሉም	5
ማንኛውም የስጦታ እቃ ተስፋ አደርጋለሁ	5
የስጦታ እቃ የሚሰጥበት ተስፋ አደርጋለሁ	6
የስጦታ እቃ አንደሚሆን ተስፋ አደርጋለሁ	6
የስጦታ እቃ አንደሚተካ ተስፋ አደርጋለሁ	6
የስጦታ እቃ አንደደረሰ ተስፋ አደርጋለሁ	6
የስጦታ እቃ አንደሚወጣ ተስፋ አደርጋለሁ	6
የስጦታ እቃ አንደሚመጣ ተስፋ አደርጋለሁ	6
የስጦታ እቃ አንደሚጠጣ ተስፋ አደርጋለሁ	6

Table 4: Sample n-gram based suggestion for a sentence "የስጦታ እቃ -ተዘነጉ ተስፋ አደርጋለሁ".

If the edit distance is the same as a different suggestion, then the decision is made by selecting the one that result lower perplexity.

Accordingly, the phrase "የስጦታ እቃ ተስፋ አደርጋለሁ ብለዋል" selected due to better perplexity of language model.

Similarly, Table 5 presents sample Amharic speech recognition output along with the corrected sentence using our post-edit technique.

No	Type	Sentence recognized and corrected
1	Raw	አራስን ጭምሮ ጉብኝት እገዛ+ ዋጋ ይኖረል
	Edited	አራስን ጭምሮ ጉብኝት በዚ ዋጋ ይኖረል
2	Raw	አባክዎን ተሽካሚ+ ጥሩት
	Edited	አባክዎን ተሽካሚውን ጥሩት
3	Raw	አባኮን+ ሌላ ፎጣ ማግኘት እችላለሁ
	Edited	አባክዎን ሌላ ፎጣ ማግኘት እችላለሁ
4	Raw	አባክዎን ሻንጣዎን ይክፈቱ+
	Edited	አባክዎን ሻንጣዎን ይክፈቱት
5	Raw	የስጦታ እቃ +ግዘት እያሱብኩ ነው
	Edited	የስጦታ እቃ ለመግዘት እያሱብኩ ነው
6	Raw	ይህ የጉዞ ላይ ህመም -ያጋጥም ይችላል
	Edited	ይህ የጉዞ ላይ ህመም ሊያጋጥም ይችላል
7	Raw	-ህ ባቡር ዶቫር በስንት ሰኣት ይደርሳል
	Edited	ይህ ባቡር ዶቫር በስንት ሰኣት ይደርሳል
8	Raw	ሻንጣዎን ይክፈቱ -ም
	Edited	ሻንጣዎን ይክፈቱ
9	Raw	አባክዎን ተሽካሚውን +ጥሩት
	Edited	አባክዎን ተሽካሚውን ይጥሩት

Table 5: Sample corrected sentences of Amharic speech recognizer.

6 Experimental results

Speech translation experiments are conducted through cascading components of speech translation as discussed in Section 1. In speech recognition experiments, Kaldi (Povey et al., 2011), SRILM (Stolcke et al., 2002) and Morfessor 2.0 (Smit et al., 2014) have been used for Amharic speech recognition, language modeling and unsupervised segmentation, respectively.

Morfessor based segmentation has been applied to segment training, testing and language model data for Amharic. In addition to this, Moses and MGIZA++ for implementing a phrase based statistical machine translation and Python is used for implementing the post-edit algorithm and to integrate ASR and SMT under the Linux platform.

The entire ASR experiment is conducted using a morpheme-based language model with phoneme-based acoustic model. Accordingly, the experimental result is computed using NIST Scoring Toolkit (SCTK)[5] and presented in terms of word recognition accuracy (WRA[6]) and morph recognition accuracy (MRA).

Thus, the Amharic speech recognition experiment shows a 76.4% for the morpheme-based. Then, after the concatination of morphemes to words, a 77.4% word-based recognition accuracy have been achieved.

Consequently, Amharic-English SMT experiment have been conducted with and without considering Amharic ASR result.

The first two experiments were conducted without considering ASR. Accordingly, a word-word system resulted in a BLEU score of 14.72 while morpheme-word brings about 11.24 BLEU. Combining Amharic ASR with Amharic-English SMT as cascading component resulted in a 6.29 BLEU score through 76.4% of recognition accuracy for Amharic morpheme and English word based translation.

Similarly, Amharic word with English word based translation shows a 12.83 BLEU score using 77.4% recognition accuracy without using ASR post-edit. The result achieved by ASR can further be improved by applying post-edit on Amharic speech recognition.

---

[5]evaluation toolkit available at http://my.fit.edu/~vkepuska/ece5527/sctk-2.3-rc1/doc/sctk.htm

[6]WRA is obtained by concatenating the result obtained by MRA

Table 6 depicts Amaharic-English speech translation before and after Amharic ASR post-edit.

	Before		After
	Morpheme	Word	Word
ASR (%)	76.4	77.4	78.5
SMT (in BLEU)	6.29	12.83	13.08

Table 6: Amharic-English Speech Translation result.

Accordingly, the morpheme based recognition followed by post-edit resulted in a BLEU score of 13.08 at 78.5% of word recognition accuracy speech translation.

The result obtained from the n-gram post-edit experiment shows an absolute advance by 1.42% from word recognition accuracy of 77.4% obtained by concatenating a 76.4% morpheme based recognition. Similarly, BLEU score evaluation advanced by 1.95% (from 12.83 to 13.08).

7 Conclussion and Future work

Speech translation research has been studied for more than a decade for resourced and technological supported languages like English, European and Asian. On the contrary, attempts for under resourced languages, not yet started, particularly for Amharic. This paper presents the first Amharic speech to English text translation using the cascading components of speech translation.

For ASR, a 20 hours of training and 7.43 hours of testing speech were used consuming a morpheme-based language model with a phonemic acoustic model. Whereas for SMT, 19,472 sentence for training and 8112 sentences for testing used. Similarly to apply ASR post-edit using n-gram approach, a corpus consisting 681,910 sentences were used.

Accordingly, speech translation through ASR post-editing resulted a 0.25 (1.95%) BLEU score enhancement from the word-based SMT. The enhancement seemed as a result of improving ASR by 1.42% using a corpus based n-gram post-edit.

The current study shows the possibility of enhancing the performance of speech translation by controlling speech recognition error propagation using post-editing algorithm.

Further works need to be done to apply post-editing both at the recognition and the translation stages of speech translation.

References

Solomon Teferra Abate, Wolfgang Menzel, Bairu Tafila, et al. 2005. An amharic speech corpus for large vocabulary continuous speech recognition. In *INTERSPEECH*, pages 1601–1604.

Tadesse Anberbir and Tomio Takara. 2009. Development of an amharic text-to-speech system using cepstral method. In *Proceedings of the First Workshop on Language Technologies for African Languages*, pages 46–52. Association for Computational Linguistics.

Laurent Besacier, V-B Le, Christian Boitet, and Vincent Berment. 2006. Asr and translation for under-resourced languages. In *Acoustics, Speech and Signal Processing, 2006. ICASSP 2006 Proceedings. 2006 IEEE International Conference on*, volume 5, pages V–V. IEEE.

David Blachon, Elodie Gauthier, Laurent Besacier, Guy-Noël Kouarata, Martine Adda-Decker, and Annie Rialland. 2016. Parallel speech collection for under-resourced language studies using the ligaikuma mobile device app. *Procedia Computer Science*, 81:61–66.

Yuqing Gao, Liang Gu, Bowen Zhou, Ruhi Sarikaya, Mohamed Afify, Hong-Kwang Kuo, Wei-zhong Zhu, Yonggang Deng, Charles Prosser, Wei Zhang, et al. 2006. Ibm mastor system: Multilingual automatic speech-to-speech translator. In *Proceedings of the Workshop on Medical Speech Translation*, pages 53–56. Association for Computational Linguistics.

Elodie Gauthier, Laurent Besacier, Sylvie Voisin, Michael Melese, and Uriel Pascal Elingui. 2016. Collecting resources in sub-saharan african languages for automatic speech recognition: a case study of wolof. In *Proceedings of the Tenth International Conference on Language Resources and Evaluation LREC 2016, Portorož, Slovenia, May 23-28, 2016*.

Masaaki Honda. 2003. Human speech production mechanisms. *NTT Technical Review*, 1(2):24–29.

Daniel Jurafsky and James H Martin. 2008. *Speech and language processing (prentice hall series in artificial intelligence)*. Prentice Hall.

Fondazione Bruno Kessler. 2010. A generic weaver for supporting product lines. In *International Workshop on Spoken Language Translation*, pages 11–18. ACM.

Akira Kurematsu. 1996. *Automatic Speech Translation*, volume 28. CRC Press.

Michael Melese, Laurent Besacier, and Million Meshesha. 2016. Amharic speech recognition for speech translation. In *Atelier Traitement Automatique des Langues Africaines (TALAF). JEP-TALN 2016*.

Satoshi Nakamura. 2009. Overcoming the language barrier with speech translation technology. *Science & Technology Trends-Quarterly Review*, (31).

Daniel Povey, Arnab Ghoshal, Gilles Boulianne, Lukas Burget, Ondrej Glembek, Nagendra Goel, Mirko Hannemann, Petr Motlicek, Yanmin Qian, Petr Schwarz, et al. 2011. The kaldi speech recognition toolkit. In *IEEE 2011 workshop on automatic speech recognition and understanding*, EPFL-CONF-192584. IEEE Signal Processing Society.

Gary F. Simons and Charles D. Fennig. 2017. *Ethnologue: Languages of the World*. SIL, Dallas, Texas.

Peter Smit, Sami Virpioja, Stig-Arne Gronroos, and Mikko Kurimo. 2014. Morfessor 2.0: Toolkit for statistical morphological segmentation. In *14th Conference of the European Chapter of the Association for Computational Linguistics*, pages 21–24. European Chapter of the Association for Computational Linguistics, EACL.

Andreas Stolcke et al. 2002. Srilm-an extensible language modeling toolkit. Interspeech.

Martha Yifiru Tachbelie and Solomon Teferra Abate. 2015. Effect of language resources on automatic speech recognition for amharic. In *AFRICON, 2015*, pages 1–5. IEEE.

Mulu Gebreegziabher Teshome, Laurent Besacier, Girma Taye, and Dereje Teferi. 2015. Phoneme-based english-amharic statistical machine translation. In *AFRICON, 2015*, pages 1–5. IEEE.

Irene Thompson. 2016. About world language. Accessed: 2017-05-26.

UNWTO. 2016. World tourism organization annual report 2015. Technical report, United Nation, Madrid, Spain.

Baye Yimam. 2000. *Yeamarigna sewasew (Amharic version)*. EMPDA, Addis Ababa, Ethiopia.

Speech- and Text-driven Features
for Automated Scoring of English Speaking Tasks

Anastassia Loukina   **Nitin Madnani**   **Aoife Cahill**

Educational Testing Service
Princeton, NJ, 08541 USA
`{aloukina,nmadnani,acahill}@ets.org`

Abstract

We consider the automatic scoring of a task for which both the content of the response as well the pronunciation and fluency are important. We combine features from a text-only content scoring system originally designed for written responses with several categories of acoustic features. Although adding any single category of acoustic features to the text-only system on its own does not significantly improve performance, adding *all* acoustic features together does yield a small but significant improvement. These results are consistent for responses to open-ended questions and to questions focused on some given source material.

1 Introduction

English language proficiency assessments designed to evaluate speaking ability often include tasks that require the test takers to speak for one or two minutes on a particular topic. These responses are then evaluated by a human rater in terms of how well the test takers addressed the question as well as the general proficiency of their speech. Therefore, a system designed to automatically score such responses should combine NLP components aimed at evaluating the content of the response as well as text-based aspects of speaking proficiency such as vocabulary and grammar, and speech-processing components aimed at evaluating fluency and pronunciation. In this paper, we investigate the automatic scoring of such spoken responses collected as part of a large-scale assessment of English speaking ability.

Our corpus contains responses to two types of questions — both administered as part of the same speaking ability task — that we will refer to as "source-based" and "general". For source-based questions, test-takers are expected to use the provided materials (e.g., a reading passage) as a basis for their response and, therefore, good responses are likely to have similar content. In contrast, general questions are more open-ended such as "What is your favorite food and why?" and, therefore, the content of such responses can vary greatly across test takers. In total, our corpus contains over 150,000 spoken responses to 147 different questions, both source-based and general.

We focus our system on two dimensions of proficiency: content, that is how well the test-taker addressed the task, and delivery (pronunciation and fluency). To evaluate the content of a spoken response, we use features from an existing content-scoring NLP system developed for written responses that uses the textual characteristics of the response to produce a score. We apply this system to the 1-best ASR (automatic speech recognition) hypotheses for the spoken responses.

To evaluate the fluency and pronunciation of the speech in the response, we use features from an existing speech-scoring system that capture information relevant to spoken language proficiency and cannot be obtained just from the ASR hypothesis. We compare the contributions of several types of features: speech rate, pausing patterns, pronunciation measures based on acoustic model scores and ASR confidence scores as well as more complex features that capture timing patterns and other prosodic properties of the response.

We combine the two types of features (text-driven and speech-driven) and compare the performance of this model to two baseline models, each using only one type of features. All models are evaluated by comparing the scores obtained from that model to the scores assigned by human raters to the same responses. We hypothesize that:

67

Proceedings of the First Workshop on Speech-Centric Natural Language Processing, pages 67–77
Copenhagen, Denmark, September 7–11, 2017. ©2017 Association for Computational Linguistics

- Given the characteristics of the two types of questions, the model with *only* text-driven features will exhibit better performance for source-based questions as opposed to general ones.

- Since human raters reward how well the response addresses the question as well as higher spoken proficiency, the combined model that uses *both* text-driven features (for content) & speech-driven features (for proficiency) will perform better than the individual text-only and speech-only models.

We find that our results generally meet our expectations but interestingly the improvement in performance by combining text-driven & speech-driven features — while significant — is not as large as we had expected, i.e., the combination does not add much over the text-driven features. We conclude by discussing possible reasons for this observation.

2 Related work

Most systems for scoring proficiency of spoken responses rely on ASR to obtain a transcription of the responses. Since work on automated scoring predates the availability of accurate ASR, the majority of earlier automated scoring systems focused on tasks that elicited restricted speech such as read-aloud or repeat-aloud. Such systems either did not consider the content of the response at all or relied on relatively simple string-matching (see Eskenazi (2009) and Zechner et al. (2009) for a detailed review). Even when the task required answering open-ended questions, e.g. in the PhonePass test (Townshend et al., 1998; Bernstein et al., 2000), fluency was considered more important than content.

Zechner et al. (2009) were one of the first to attempt automatically scoring tasks that not only elicited open-ended responses but where content knowledge was also an integral part of the task. They did not use any explicit features to measure content because of the high ASR word error rates (around 50%). Instead, they focused on fluency-related features on which ASR errors had little impact. They reported a correlation of 0.62 between the system and human scores.

More recent studies have explored different approaches to evaluating the content of spoken responses. Xie et al. (2012) explored content mea-

sures based on the lexical similarity between the response and a set of reference responses. A content-scoring component based on word vectors was also part of the automated scoring engine described by Cheng et al. (2014). In both these studies, content features were developed to supplement other features measuring various aspects of speaking proficiency. Neither study reported the relative contributions of content and speech features to the system performance.

Although it may seem obvious that, given the nature of the task, a model using both speech-based and content-based features should outperform models using only one of them, it may not turn out that way. Multiple studies that have developed new features measuring vocabulary, grammar or content for spoken responses have reported only limited improvements when these features were combined with features based on fluency and pronunciation (Bhat and Yoon, 2015; Yoon et al., 2012; Somasundaran et al., 2015). Crossley and McNamara (2013) used a large set of text-based measures including Coh-Metrix (Graesser et al., 2004) to obtain fairly accurate predictions of proficiency scores for spoken responses to general questions similar to the ones used in this study based on transcription only, without using any information based on acoustic analysis of speech. It is not possible to establish from published results how their system would compare to the one that also evaluates pronunciation and fluency. They did not compute any such features and their results based on text are not directly comparable to the other papers discussed in this section since some of their features required a minimum length of 100 words and, therefore, required them to combine several responses to meet this text length requirement.

Most recently, Loukina and Cahill (2016) compared the performance of several text- and speech-based scoring systems and found that even though each system individually achieved reasonable accuracy in predicting proficiency scores, there was no improvement in performance from combining the systems. They argued that the majority of speakers who perform well along one dimension of language proficiency are also likely to perform well along other dimensions (cf. also Xi (2007) who reports similar results for human analytic scores). Consequently, the gain in performance from combining different systems is small or nonexistent. Their work focused on general language proficiency features and did not consider the content of the responses.

This study has several significant differences from previous work. We consider content-scoring features that go well beyond word vectors and instead build a textual profile of the response. Furthermore, we conduct more fine-grained analyses and report the *types* of speech-driven features that add the most information to content-scoring features. We also examine how the interactions between content and speech features vary by types of questions. Finally, we conduct our analyses on a very large corpus of spoken responses which, to our knowledge, is the largest used so far in studies on automated scoring of spoken responses. The size of the data allows us to identify patterns that persist across responses to multiple questions and are more reliable.

3 Methodology

3.1 Data

The data used in this study comes from a large-scale English proficiency assessment for non-native speakers administered in multiple countries. Each test-taker answers up to 6 questions: two general and four source-based. For source-based questions, test-takers are provided with spoken and/or written materials and asked to respond to a question based on these materials while general questions have no such materials. Test-takers are given 45 seconds to answer general questions and one minute to answer source-based questions.

Each response was scored by a professional human rater on a scale of 1–4. When assigning scores, raters evaluated both how well the test taker addressed the task in terms of content as well as the overall intelligibility of the speech. A response scored as a "1" would be limited in content and/or largely intelligible due to consistent pronunciation difficulties and limited use of vocabulary and grammar. On the other hand, a response scored as a "4" would fulfill the demands of the task and be highly intelligible with clear speech and effective use of grammar and vocabulary. The raters are provided with the description of typical responses at each score level and are asked to provide a holistic score without prioritizing any particular aspect.

For this study, we used responses to 147 questions (48 general questions and 99 source-

Type	general	source-based
N questions	48	99
N responses	50,811	102,650
Average responses	1058.6	1036.9
Median responses	902.5	936.0
Min responses	255	250
Max responses	2030	2,174
Average N words	90.8	120.3

Table 1: Total number of responses for each question type; the average, median, min and max number of responses per question; the average number of words in responses to each question computed based on ASR hypotheses.

based questions) from different administrations of the assessment. We excluded responses where the ASR hypothesis contained fewer than 10 words (0.2% of the original sample). The final corpus used for model training and evaluation included 153,461 responses from 33,503 test takers.[1] As shown in Table 1, the number of responses for a question was consistent for the two question types.

Test-takers from each administration were randomly split between training and evaluation partition with about 70% of responses to each question allocated to the training set and 30% allocated to the evaluation set. We ensured that, across all 147 questions, responses from the same test taker were *always* allocated to the same partition and that test takers in training and evaluation sets had similar demographic characteristics.

3.2 Automatic Speech Recognizer

All responses were processed using an automatic speech-recognition system based on the Kaldi toolkit (Povey et al., 2011) using the approach described by Tao et al. (2016). The language model was based on tri-grams. The acoustic models were based on 5-layer DNN and 13 MFCC-based features. Tao et al. (2016) give further detail about the model training procedure.

The ASR system was trained on a proprietary corpus consisting of 800 hours of non-native speech from 8,700 speakers of more than 100 native languages. The speech in the ASR training

---

[1] Our sampling was done by question and some questions were repeated across administrations in combination with other questions not included in this study. The number of speakers who answered each question varied between 250 and 2,174, with an average of 1,043 responses to each question. For 68% of test takers, we had responses to all 6 questions.

corpus was elicited using questions similar to the ones considered in this study. There was no overlap of speakers or questions between the ASR training corpus and the corpus used in this paper. We did not additionally adapt the ASR to the speakers or responses in this study.

While no transcriptions are available to compute the WER of the ASR system on this corpus, the WER for this system on a similar corpus is around 30%.

3.3 Text-driven features

Scoring responses for writing quality requires measuring whether the student can organize and develop an argument and write fluently with no grammatical errors or misspellings. In contrast, scoring for content deals with responses to open-ended questions designed to test what the student knows, has learned, or can do in a specific subject area (such as Computer Science, Math, or Biology) (Sukkarieh and Stoyanchev, 2009; Sukkarieh, 2011; Mohler et al., 2011; Dzikovska et al., 2013; Ramachandran et al., 2015; Sakaguchi et al., 2015; Zhu et al., 2016).[2]

In order to measure the content of the spoken responses in our data, we extract the following set of features from the 1-best ASR hypotheses for each response:

- lowercased word n-grams (n=1,2), including punctuation

- lowercased character n-grams (n=2,3,4,5)

- syntactic dependency triples computed using the ZPar parser (Zhang and Clark, 2011)

- length bins (specifically, whether the log of 1 plus the number of characters in the response, rounded down to the nearest integer, equals x, for all possible x from the training set). For example, consider a question for which transcriptions of the responses in the training data are between 50 and 200 characters long. For this question, we will have 3 length bins numbered from 5 ($\lfloor \log_2 51 \rfloor$) to 7 ($\lfloor \log_2 201 \rfloor$). For a new response of length 150 characters, length bin 7 ($\lfloor \log_2 151 \rfloor$) would be the binary feature that gets a value of 1 with the other two bins getting the value of 0.

We refer to these features as "text-driven" features in subsequent sections.

---

[2]See Table 3 in Burrows et al. (2015) for a detailed list.

3.4 Speech-driven features

We used five types of features that capture information relevant to the fluency and pronunciation of a spoken response and are extracted based on the acoustic properties of the spoken responses. These are primarily related to spectral quality (*how* the words and sounds were pronounced) and timing (*when* they were pronounced). All features are summarized in Table 2. Each feature type is computed as a continuous value for the whole response and relies on the availability of *both* the speech signal as well as the 1-best ASR hypothesis.

The first set of features ("speech rate") computes the words spoken per minute with and without trailing and leading pauses. Speech rate has been consistently identified as one of the major covariates of language proficiency and the features in this group have some of the highest correlations with the overall human score.

Name	Description	N_{feat}	r
speech rate	Speech rate	3	.42
quality	Segmental quality	6	.41
pausing	Location and duration of pauses	9	.34
timing	Patterns of durations of individual segments	9	.36
prosody	Time intervals between stressed syllables	6	.30

Table 2: The five sets of speech features used in this study along with the number of features in each group and the average correlations with human score across all features and questions (Pearson's r).

The second set of features ("quality") captures how much the pronunciation of individual segments deviates from the pronunciation that would be expected from a proficient speaker. This includes the average confidence scores and acoustic model scores computed by the ASR system for the words in the 1-best ASR hypothesis. Since the ASR is trained on a wide range of proficiency levels, we also include features computed using the two-pass approach (Herron et al., 1999; Chen et al., 2009). In this approach, the acoustic model scores for words in the ASR hypothesis are recomputed using acoustic models trained on native speakers of English.

The third set of features captures pausing patterns in the response such as mean duration of pauses, mean number of words between two pauses, and the ratio of pauses to speech. For all features in this group the pauses were determined based on silences in the ASR output. Only silences longer than 0.145 seconds were included.

The fourth set of features ("prosody") measures patterns of variation in time intervals between stressed syllables as well as the number of syllables between adjacent stressed syllables (Zechner et al., 2011).

The final set of features ("timing") captures variation in the duration of vowels and consonants. This category includes features such as relative proportion of vocalic intervals or variability in adjacent consonantal intervals (Lai et al., 2013; Chen and Zechner, 2011) as well as features which compare vowel duration to reference models trained on native speakers (Chen et al., 2009).

We refer to these five feature sets as "speech-driven" features in subsequent sections.

3.5 Scoring models

We combined the text-driven features and speech-driven features into a single set of features and trained a support vector regressor (SVR) model with an RBF kernel for each of the 147 questions, using the human scores in the training partition as the labels. We used the *scikit-learn* (Pedregosa et al., 2011) implementation of SVRs and the SKLL toolkit.[3] The hyper-parameters of each SVR model (γ and C) were optimized using a cross-validated search over a grid with mean squared error (MSE) as the objective function.

In addition to the combined scoring models, we also built the following scoring models for each question:

- A model using only the text-driven features (1 model)

- A model using only the speech-driven features (1 model)

- Models using each of the individual speech-driven feature sets (5 models)

- Combinations of the text-driven model with each of the individual speech-driven feature sets (5 models)

[3]http://github.com/
EducationalTestingService/skll

In total, we built 1,911 scoring models (13 models for each of the 147 questions).

We evaluated each of our models on a held-out evaluation partition for each of the questions. We used the R^2 between the predicted and human scores computed on the evaluation set as a measure of model performance:

$$R^2 = 1 - \frac{\sum (y_i - \hat{y}_i)^2}{\sum (y_i - \bar{y})^2} \quad (1)$$

where y_i are the observed values (human scores), $\hat{y}_i$ are the predicted values and $\bar{y}$ is the mean of observed scores.

As shown in Eq. 1, R^2 standardizes the MSE by the total variance of the observed values leading to a more interpretable metric that generally varies from 0 to 1, where 1 corresponds to perfect prediction and 0 indicates that the model is no more accurate than simply using mean value as the prediction.

4 Results

4.1 Model performance

Table 3 shows the mean R^2 for different types of questions and models across the 147 questions in our study.

Model	general	source-based
text + speech	.352	.442
text-only	.335	.431
speech-only	.325	.394
speech rate	.275	.341
pausing	.259	.312
quality	.303	.365
prosody	.256	.309
timing	.282	.329
text + speech rate	.339	.433
text + pausing	.340	.434
text + quality	.343	.436
text + prosody	.341	.434
text + timing	.342	.434

Table 3: Average R^2 achieved by different models on different types of questions (N=99 for general questions and N=48 for source-based questions).

We used linear mixed-effect models (cf. Snijders and Bosker (2012) for a comprehensive introduction and Searle et al. (1992) who give an extensive historical overview) to identify statistically significant differences among the various models. The mixed-effect models were fitted using the `statsmodels` Python package (Seabold and Perktold, 2010). We used model R^2 as a dependent variable, question as a random factor, and model and question type (general or source-based) as fixed effects. We include both the main effects of model and question type as well as their interaction and used the text-driven model as the reference category.

We observed that for both general and source-based questions:

1. The performance of the combined model (text + speech) using all five types of speech-driven features as well as the text-driven features was significantly better than both the text-only model as well as the speech-only model. The effect size of the improvement over the text-only model was small with the average R^2 increasing only slightly from .335 to .352 for source-based questions and from .431 to .442 for general questions ($p = 0.002$).

2. The performance of the text-only model was significantly better than the performance of each of the 5 models trained using only one group of speech-driven features ($p < 0.0001$).

3. There was no significant difference between the performance of the text-only model and the 5 models combining the text-driven features with each of the individual speech-driven feature sets.

In addition, as we predicted, there was a significant difference in model performance between general and source-based questions. Surprisingly, this difference was observed for *all* 13 models; all models achieved higher performance for source-based questions ($p < 0.0001$). We also observed a significant interaction between model type and question type: the difference between the speech-only model and the text-only model was higher for source-based questions than for general questions. Furthermore, while there was no statistically significant difference between the speech-only model and text-only model for general questions (.335 vs. .325, p=0.061), the difference between these two types of models *was* significant for source-based questions with the text-only model outperforming the speech-only model (R^2 = .431 vs. .394, $p < 0.0001$).

Finally, we compared the performance of our combined system to other published results on automated speech scoring reviewed earlier in this paper. Since most previous work reports their results using Pearson's correlation coefficients, we computed the same for our system for an easier comparison. Table 4 reports the correlations for our model as well as those reported in previous studies on automatically scoring responses to similar questions. It shows that our system performance is either comparable or better than previous results.

Model	general	source-based
text + speech	.60	.67
text-only	.59	.66
speech-only	.58	.63
Xie et al.	.40	.59
Loukina & Cahill	.64 (overall)	

Table 4: Average Pearson's r achieved by the three of the models in this study and the best performing models reported in the literature; Loukina and Cahill (2016) combine language proficiency features from speech and text and do not report performance by question type; Xie et al. (2012) use content features based on cosine similarity but no other language proficiency features. If a paper reports results based on both ASR hypothesis and human transcription, we only use the results based on ASR hypothesis.

4.2 Information overlap between text and speech: The role of disfluencies

A relatively minor improvement between the text-only model and the combined text + speech model suggests that text-driven features already incorporate some of the information captured by the speech-driven features or that the type of of information captured by two sets of features are highly correlated. We use disfluencies and pauses as a test case to explore this hypothesis further.

Our text-driven features computed on the ASR hypothesis included *all* information stored in that hypothesis including hesitation markers ("uh", "uhm" etc.) and silence markers. In other words, even though our text-driven features are designed to measure content for written responses, when applied to spoken responses they might also have captured some information related to fluency. In order to confirm this hypothesis, we removed hesitation markers and pauses from the 1-best ASR hypotheses and repeated our analysis with the primary models, i.e., text-only (with and without disfluencies), speech-only, and text + speech (with and without disfluencies) – a total of 5 models.

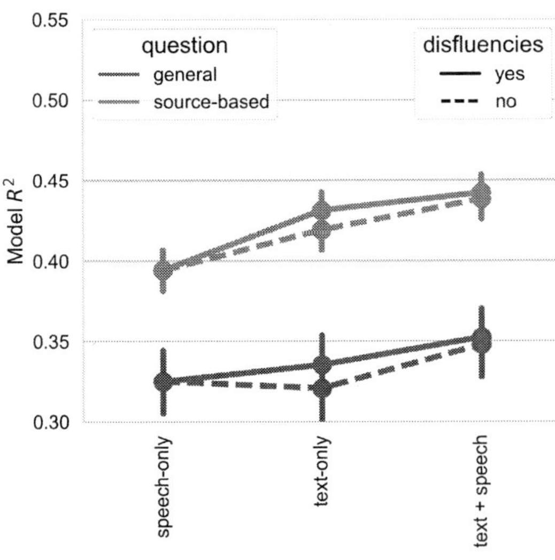

Figure 1: A plot showing the scoring performance across the two question types for two different conditions: including disfluencies and pauses in the 1-best ASR hypotheses and excluding them.

The results of this analysis are presented in Figure 1. As before, we used a linear mixed-effects model to evaluate which differences were statistically significant. Removing disfluencies and pauses from the hypotheses led to a significant decrease in the performance of the text-only model for both types of questions (R^2 = .335 vs. .321 for general question and .431 vs. .419 for source-based questions, $p = 0.001$).

We still observed no significant difference in performance between the text-only model without disfluencies and pauses and speech-only model for *general* questions. However, the difference between the text-only model and speech-only models for *source-based* questions remained significant even after removing the disfluencies and pauses from the ASR hypothesis (.394 vs. .419, $p < 0.001$).

Finally, for the combined text + speech model, there was no significant difference between including and excluding disfluencies and pauses from the ASR hypotheses.

4.3 Performance variation across questions

In Section 4.1, we presented general observations after we controlled for the individual question as a random effect. However, we also observed that all of the models showed substantial variation in performance across the 147 questions. The R^2 for the best performing model (text + speech) varied between .062 and .505 for the general questions and between .197 and .557 for the source-based questions. Given such a striking variation, we conducted further exploratory analyses into factors that may have affected model performance. We focused these analyses on the best performing model (text + speech).

First, we considered the sample size for each question. As shown in Table 1, the number of responses used to train and evaluate the models varied across questions and, therefore, we might expect lower performance for questions with fewer responses available for model training. A linear regression model with R^2 as the dependent variable and the sample size as the independent variable showed that the sample size accounted for 9.8% of variability in model performance for source-based questions ($p = 0.0016$) and 19.2% of variability in model performance for general questions ($p = 0.0018$). In other words, while there was a significant effect of the sample size, it was not the main factor.

Another possible source of variation in model performance may be the variation in ASR word error rate itself. Since no reference transcriptions are available for our corpus, we cannot test this hypothesis directly. As an indirect measurement, however, we consider the number of words in the ASR hypotheses across questions. If the ASR consistently failed to produce accurate hypotheses for some questions, this might manifest as consistently shorter ASR hypothesis for such questions, and, hence, discrepant scoring performance.

The average number of words varied between 83.6 and 100.2 for general questions and between 109.0 and 132.6 for source-based questions. While there was a statistically significant difference in number of words between the questions, we found that the average number of words in responses to a given question did not have a significant effect on the model performance ($p = 0.09$ for general questions and $p = 0.03$ for source-based questions[4]).

---

[4] Significance threshold was adjusted for multiple compar-

Of course, not all ASR failures necessarily result in shorter hypotheses and, therefore, further analysis based on the actual WER is necessary to reject or confirm any possible effect of ASR on model performance.

There are additional factors that might have contributed to the variation in model performance pertaining to both the properties of the question and the characteristics of test takers who answered each question. We plan to further explore the contribution of these factors in future work. Our results highlight the impact of the actual question in automated scoring studies and suggest that the results based on a small set of questions may be unreliable due to the large variation across questions.

5 Discussion

We considered a combination of text-driven and speech-driven features for automated scoring of spoken responses to general and source-based questions. We found that for both types of questions a combination of the two types of features outperforms models using only one of those two types of features. However, a significant improvement could only be achieved by combining several types of speech features. There was no improvement in model performance when text-driven features were combined with only one type of speech-driven features such as speech rate or pausing patterns.

Surprisingly we found that all models performed better for source-based questions than for general questions — a result we plan to explore further in future work. We also found that for general questions where the content of responses can vary greatly, the model that uses only speech-driven features achieves the same performance as the one only using text-driven features. We hypothesize that this is because in the absence of "pre-defined" content both systems measure various aspects of general linguistic proficiency and these tend to be closely related as we discussed in Section 2. At the same time, for source-based questions where the test-takers are expected to cover already provided content, the performance of the model using only text-driven features is significantly better than the performance of the model using only speech-driven features.

Although we do observe a significant improve-

ment in scoring performance by combining text-driven features (to measure content) and speech-driven features (to measure fluency and pronunciation), the improvement is not as large as one might have expected. This may appear counter-intuitive considering the perceived role of fluency and pronunciation for this task. There are several possible reasons for this result.

First, it is possible that the speech-driven features in our study do not really capture the information present in the acoustic signal that is relevant to this task. However, this is unlikely given that the features we considered in this paper capture many aspects of spoken language proficiency and cover all major types of features used in other studies on automated evaluation of spoken proficiency. This is further illustrated by the fact that for general questions, the speech-only model performed as well as the text-only model. We also note that recent work by Yu et al. (2016) used neural networks to learn high-level abstractions from frame-to-frame acoustic properties of the signal and showed that these features provided a very limited gain over the features considered in this study.

Second, our results may be skewed because of poorly performing ASR. Although we cannot reject this hypothesis given the lack of human transcriptions for the responses, it is unlikely to hold because the same ASR system achieves a WER of 30% on another corpus of responses with similar demographic and response characteristics. Furthermore, previous studies compared the performance of speech and text features computed using manual transcriptions to those computed using ASR hypotheses (with a similar WER) and reported only a small drop in performance: $r = 0.67$ for transcriptions vs. $r = 0.64$ for ASR hypotheses (Loukina and Cahill, 2016).

Another possible reason may be the way in which the speech-driven and text-driven features are combined. For each response, we simply concatenate the small, dense vector of 33 continuous speech-driven features with the very large, sparse vector of tens of thousands of binary text-driven features. In such a scenario, the impact of speech-driven features may be mitigated due to the disproportionate number of sparse text-driven features. A better combination approach might be stacked generalization (Wolpert, 1992): building separate models for speech-driven features and text-driven

---

isons performed in this section to $\alpha = 0.0125$ using Bonferroni correction

features and then combining their predictions in a third higher-level model. Sakaguchi et al. (2015) showed that stacking only improves over straightforward concatenation when there are a limited number of responses in the training data and we have a fairly large number of training responses available for each of our questions. However, the idea certainly merits further exploration.

A more likely explanation is that there is only a limited amount of information contained in the acoustic signal that is not already present in one way or another in the ASR hypothesis. We already discussed earlier in this paper that different aspects of language proficiency are highly correlated and thus one model can often achieve good empirical performance by measuring only one particular aspect. A related observation here is that many aspects of the spoken signal are already captured by ASR hypothesis. For example, while ASR hypothesis does not reflect the duration of pauses, it does contain information about the presence and location of pauses and whether they are accompanied by the hesitation markers. Similarly, the "choppiness" of speech would manifest itself in both prosody and syntax. This claim is supported by our results which show that removing disfluencies and pauses from the ASR hypotheses degrades the performance of the text-only system significantly but has no effect on the performance of the combined system since the same information is also captured by the speech-driven features.

In this study, we focused on content, fluency, and pronunciation and did not consider any features designed to measure other important elements of speaking proficiency such as grammar or choice of vocabulary. It is likely that some aspects of these are already indirectly captured by the content-scoring part of our system but future research will show whether system performance can be further improved by features that have been specifically designed to evaluate these aspects of spoken proficiency.

6 Conclusions

In this paper, we built automated scoring models for an English speaking task for which both content knowledge as well as an ability to produce fluent intelligible speech are required in order to obtain a high score. We applied an existing content-scoring NLP system (designed for written responses) to the 1-best ASR hypotheses of the spoken responses in order to extract text-driven features that measure content. To measure spoken fluency and pronunciation, we extracted a set of 33 features based on the acoustic signal for the response. Combining the two types of features results in a significant but smaller than expected improvement compared to using each type of features by itself. A deeper examination of the features yields that there is likely to be significant information overlap between the speech signal and the ASR 1-best hypothesis especially when the hypothesis includes pausing and silence markers. Based on these observations, we conclude that although our approach of extracting features from the speech signal and combining them with text-driven features extracted from the ASR hypothesis is certainly moderately effective, further research is warranted in order to determine whether a larger improvement can be obtained for this task.

Acknowledgments

We would like to thank Keelan Evanini, Su-Youn Yoon, Brian Riordan, and the anonymous SCNLP reviewers for their useful comments and suggestions. We also thank Matt Mulholland for help with processing the data.

References

Jared Bernstein, John De Jong, David B. Pisoni, and Brent Townshend. 2000. Two experiments on automatic scoring of spoken language proficiency. In *Proceedings of InStil2000*. pages 57–61.

Suma Bhat and Su-Youn Yoon. 2015. Automatic assessment of syntactic complexity for spontaneous speech scoring. *Speech Communication* 67:42–57.

Steven Burrows, Iryna Gurevych, and Benno Stein. 2015. The eras and trends of automatic short answer grading. *International Journal of Artificial Intelligence in Education* 25(1):60–117.

Lei Chen and Klaus Zechner. 2011. Applying rhythm features to automatically assess non-native speech. In *Proceedings of Interspeech*. pages 1861–1864.

Lei Chen, Klaus Zechner, and Xiaoming Xi. 2009. Improved pronunciation features for construct-driven assessment of non-native spontaneous speech. In *Proceedings of NAACL*. pages 442–449.

Jian Cheng, Yuan Zhao D'Antilio, Xin Chen, and Jared Bernstein. 2014. Automatic assessment of the speech of young English learners. In *Proceedings of the Workshop on Innovative Use of NLP for Building Educational Applications*. pages 12–21.

Scott Crossley and Danielle McNamara. 2013. Applications of text analysis tools for spoken response grading. *Language Learning & Technology* 17(2):171–192.

Myroslava Dzikovska, Rodney Nielsen, Chris Brew, Claudia Leacock, Danilo Giampiccolo, Luisa Bentivogli, Peter Clark, Ido Dagan, and Hoa Trang Dang. 2013. Task 7: The joint student response analysis and 8th recognizing textual entailment challenge. In *Proceedings of SemEval*. pages 263–274.

Maxine Eskenazi. 2009. An overview of spoken language technology for education. *Speech Communication* 51(10):832–844.

Arthur C. Graesser, Danielle S. McNamara, Max M. Louwerse, and Zhiqiang Cai. 2004. Coh-Metrix: Analysis of text on cohesion and language. *Behavior Research Methods, Instruments, & Computers* 36(2):193–202.

Daniel Herron, Wolfgang Menzel, Eric Atwell, Roberto Bisiani, Fabio Daneluzzi, Rachel Morton, and Juergen a Schmidt. 1999. Automatic localization and diagnosis of pronunciation errors for second-language learners of English. In *Proceedings of EuroSpeech*. pages 855–858.

Catherine Lai, Keelan Evanini, and Klaus Zechner. 2013. Applying rhythm metrics to non-native spontaneous speech. In *Proceedings of SLaTE*. pages 159–163.

Anastassia Loukina and Aoife Cahill. 2016. Automated scoring across different modalities. In *Proceedings of the Workshop on Innovative Use of NLP for Building Educational Applications*. pages 130–135.

Michael Mohler, Razvan Bunescu, and Rada Mihalcea. 2011. Learning to grade short answer questions using semantic similarity measures and dependency graph alignments. In *Proceedings of ACL: HLT*. pages 752–762.

F. Pedregosa, G. Varoquaux, A. Gramfort, V. Michel, B. Thirion, O. Grisel, M. Blondel, P. Prettenhofer, R. Weiss, V. Dubourg, J. Vanderplas, A. Passos, D. Cournapeau, M. Brucher, M. Perrot, and E. Duchesnay. 2011. Scikit-learn: Machine learning in Python. *Journal of Machine Learning Research* 12:2825–2830.

Daniel Povey, Arnab Ghoshal, Gilles Boulianne, Lukas Burget, Ondrej Glembek, Nagendra Goel, Mirko Hannemann, Petr Motlicek, Yanmin Qian, Petr Schwarz, Jan Silovsky, Georg Stemmer, and Karel Vesely. 2011. The Kaldi speech recognition toolkit. In *Proceedings of the Workshop on Automatic Speech Recognition and Understanding*.

Lakshmi Ramachandran, Jian Cheng, and Peter Foltz. 2015. Identifying patterns for short answer scoring using graph-based lexico-semantic text matching. In *Proceedings of the Workshop on Innovative Use of NLP for Building Educational Applications*. pages 97–106.

Keisuke Sakaguchi, Michael Heilman, and Nitin Madnani. 2015. Effective feature integration for automated short answer scoring. In *Proceedings of NAACL*. pages 1049–1054.

Skipper Seabold and Josef Perktold. 2010. Statsmodels: Econometric and statistical modeling with Python. In *Proceedings of the Python in Science Conference*. pages 57–61.

Shayle R. Searle, George Casella, and Charles E. McCulloch. 1992. *Variance Components*. Wiley-Interscience.

Tom A.B. Snijders and Roel J. Bosker. 2012. *Multilevel Analysis*. Sage, London, 2nd edition.

Swapna Somasundaran, Chong Min Lee, Martin Chodorow, and Xinhao Wang. 2015. Automated scoring of picture-based story narration. In *Proceedings of the Workshop on Innovative Use of NLP for Building Educational Applications*. pages 42–48.

Jana Z. Sukkarieh. 2011. Using a MaxEnt classifier for the automatic content scoring of free-text responses. In *Proceedings of the 30th International Workshop on Bayesian Inference and Maximum Entropy Methods in Science and Engineering*. AIP Press, pages 41–48.

Jana Z. Sukkarieh and Svetlana Stoyanchev. 2009. Automating model building in c-rater. In *Proceedings of the Workshop on Applied Textual Inference*. pages 61–69.

Jidong Tao, Shabnam Ghaffarzadegan, Lei Chen, and Klaus Zechner. 2016. Exploring deep learning architectures for automatically grading non-native spontaneous speech. In *Proceedings of ICASSP*. pages 6140–6144.

Brent Townshend, Brent Bernstein, Ognjen Todic, and Eryk Warren. 1998. Estimation of spoken language proficiency. In *Proceedings of the Workshop on Speech Technology in Language Learning (STiLL)*. pages 93–96.

David H. Wolpert. 1992. Stacked generalization. *Neural Networks* 5:241–259.

Xiaoming Xi. 2007. Evaluating analytic scoring for the TOEFL® Academic Speaking Test (TAST) for operational use. *Language Testing* 24(2):251–286.

Shasha Xie, Keelan Evanini, and Klaus Zechner. 2012. Exploring content features for automated speech scoring. In *Proceedings of NAACL*. pages 103–111.

Su-Youn Yoon, Suma Bhat, and Klaus Zechner. 2012. Vocabulary profile as a measure of vocabulary sophistication. In *Proceedings of the Workshop on the innovative use of NLP for Building Educational Applications*. pages 180–189.

Zhou Yu, Vikram Ramanarayanan, David Suendermann-Oeft, Xinhao Wang, Klaus Zechner, Lei Chen, Jidong Tao, Aliaksei Ivanou, and Yao Qian. 2016. Using bidirectional LSTM recurrent neural networks to learn high-level abstractions of sequential features for automated scoring of non-native spontaneous speech. In *Proceedings of the IEEE Workshop on Automatic Speech Recognition and Understanding*. pages 338–345.

Klaus Zechner, Derrick Higgins, Xiaoming Xi, and David M. Williamson. 2009. Automatic scoring of non-native spontaneous speech in tests of spoken English. *Speech Communication* 51(10):883–895.

Klaus Zechner, Xiaoming Xi, and Lei Chen. 2011. Evaluating prosodic features for automated scoring of non-native read speech. In *Proceedings of the IEEE Workshop on Automatic Speech Recognition & Understanding*. pages 461–466.

Yue Zhang and Stephen Clark. 2011. Syntactic processing using the generalized perceptron and beam search. *Computational linguistics* 37(1):105–151.

Mengxiao Zhu, Ou Lydia Liu, Liyang Mao, and Amy Pallant. 2016. Use of automated scoring and feedback in online interactive Earth science tasks. In *Proceedings of the 2016 IEEE Integrated STEM Education Conference*.

Improving coreference resolution
with automatically predicted prosodic information

Ina Rösiger[*]**, Sabrina Stehwien**[*]**, Arndt Riester, Ngoc Thang Vu**
Institute for Natural Language Processing
University of Stuttgart, Germany
`{roesigia,stehwisa,arndt,thangvu}@ims.uni-stuttgart.de`

Abstract

Adding manually annotated prosodic information, specifically pitch accents and phrasing, to the typical text-based feature set for coreference resolution has previously been shown to have a positive effect on German data. Practical applications on spoken language, however, would rely on automatically predicted prosodic information. In this paper we predict pitch accents (and phrase boundaries) using a convolutional neural network (CNN) model from acoustic features extracted from the speech signal. After an assessment of the quality of these automatic prosodic annotations, we show that they also significantly improve coreference resolution.

1   Introduction

Noun phrase coreference resolution is the task of grouping noun phrases (NPs) together that refer to the same discourse entity in a text or dialogue. In Example (1), taken from Umbach (2002), the question for the coreference resolver, besides linking the anaphoric pronoun *he* back to *John*, is to decide whether *an old cottage* and *the shed* refer to the same entity.

(1) $\{$John$\}_1$ has $\{$an old cottage$\}_2$.
        Last year $\{$he$\}_1$ reconstructed $\{$the shed$\}_?$.

Coreference resolution is an active NLP research area, with its own track at most NLP conferences and several shared tasks such as the CoNLL or SemEval shared tasks (Pradhan et al., 2012; Recasens et al., 2010) or the CORBON shared task 2017[1]. Almost all work is based on text, although there exist a few systems for pronoun resolution in transcripts of spoken text (Strube and Müller, 2003; Tetreault and Allen, 2004). It has been shown that there are differences between written and spoken text that lead to a drop in performance when coreference resolution systems developed for written text are applied on spoken text (Amoia et al., 2012). For this reason, it may help to use additional information available from the speech signal, for example prosody.

In West-Germanic languages, such as English and German, there is a tendency for coreferent items, i.e. entities that have already been introduced into the discourse (their information status is *given*), to be deaccented, as the speaker assumes the entity to be salient in the listener's discourse model (cf. Terken and Hirschberg (1994); Baumann and Riester (2013); Baumann and Roth (2014)). We can make use of this fact by providing prosodic information to the coreference resolver. Example (2), this time marked with prominence information, shows that prominence can help us resolve cases where the transcription is potentially ambiguous[2].

(2) $\{$John$\}_1$ has $\{$an old cottage$\}_2$.
        a. Last year $\{$he$\}_1$ reconstructed $\{$the SHED$\}_3$.
        b. Last year $\{$he$\}_1$ reconSTRUCted **the shed**$\}_2$.

The pitch accent on *shed* in (2a) leads to the interpretation that *the shed* and *the cottage* refer to different entities, where the shed is a part of the cottage (they are in a bridging relation). In contrast, in (2b), *the shed* is deaccented, which suggests that *the shed* and *the cottage* corefer.

A pilot study by Rösiger and Riester (2015) has

---

[*]The two first authors contributed equally to this work.
[1]`http://corbon.nlp.ipipan.waw.pl/`

[2]The anaphor under consideration is typed in boldface, its antecedent is underlined. Accented syllables are capitalised.

Proceedings of the First Workshop on Speech-Centric Natural Language Processing, pages 78–83
Copenhagen, Denmark, September 7–11, 2017. ©2017 Association for Computational Linguistics

shown that enhancing the text-based feature set
for a coreference resolver, consisting of e.g. automatic part-of-speech (POS) tags and syntactic information, with pitch accents and prosodic phrasing information helps to improve coreference resolution of German spoken text. The prosodic labels used in the experiments were annotated manually, which is not only expensive but not applicable in an automatic pipeline setup. In our paper, we present an experiment in which we replicate the main results from the pilot study by annotating the prosodic information automatically, thus omitting any manual annotations from the feature set. We show that adding prosodic information significantly helps in all of our experiments.

2 Prosodic features for coreference resolution

Similar to the pilot study, we make use of *pitch accents* and *prosodic phrasing*. We predict the presence of a pitch accent[3] and use phrase boundaries to derive nuclear accents, which are taken to be the last (and perceptually most prominent) accent in an intonation phrase. This paper tests whether previously reported tendencies for manual labels are also observable for automatic labels, namely:

Short NPs Since long, complex NPs almost always have at least one pitch accent, the presence and the absence of a pitch accent is more helpful for shorter phrases.

Long NPs For long, complex NPs, we look for nuclear accents that indicate the phrase's overall prominence. If the NP contains a nuclear accent, it is assumed to be less likely to take part in coreference chains.

We test the following features that have proven beneficial in the pilot study. These features are derived for each NP.

Pitch accent presence focuses on the presence of a pitch accent, disregarding its type. If one accent is present in the NP, this boolean feature gets assigned the value *true*, and *false* otherwise.

Nuclear accent presence is a boolean feature comparable to pitch accent presence. It gets assigned the value *true* if there is a nuclear accent present in the NP, *false* otherwise.

3 Data

To ensure comparability, we use the same dataset as in the pilot study, namely the DIRNDL corpus (Eckart et al., 2012; Björkelund et al., 2014), a German radio news corpus annotated with both manual coreference and manual prosody labels. We adopt the official train, test and development split[4] designed for research on coreference resolution. The recorded news broadcasts in the DIRNDL-anaphora corpus were spoken by 13 male and 7 female speakers, in total roughly 5 hours of speech. The prosodic annotations follow the GToBI(S) standard for pitch accent types and boundary tones and are described in Björkelund et al. (2014). In this study we make use of two class labels of prosodic events: all accent types (marked by the standard ToBI *) grouped into a single class (pitch accent presence) and the same for intonational phrase boundaries (marked by %).

4 Automatic prosodic information

In this section we describe the prosodic event detector used in this work. It is a binary classifier that is trained separately for either pitch accents or phrase boundaries and predicts for each word, whether it carries the respective prosodic event.

4.1 Model

We apply a convolutional neural network (CNN) model, illustrated in Figure 1. The input to the CNN is a matrix spanning the current word and its right and left context word. The input matrix is a frame-based representation of the speech signal. The signal is divided into overlapping frames for each 20 ms with a 10 ms shift and are represented by a 6-dimensional feature vector for each frame.

We use acoustic features as well as position indicator features following Stehwien and Vu (2017) that are simple and fast to obtain. The acoustic features were extracted from the speech signal using the OpenSMILE toolkit (Eyben et al., 2013). The feature set consists of 5 features that comprise acoustic correlates of prominence: smoothed fundamental frequency (f0), RMS energy, PCM loudness, voicing probability and Harmonics-to-Noise Ratio. The position indicator feature is appended as an extra feature to the input matrices (see Figure 1) and aids the modelling of the acoustic con-

---

[3]We do not predict the pitch accent type (e.g. fall H*L or rise L*H) as this distinction was not helpful in the pilot study and is generally more difficult to model.

[4]http://www.ims.uni-stuttgart.de/
forschung/ressourcen/korpora/dirndl.
en.html

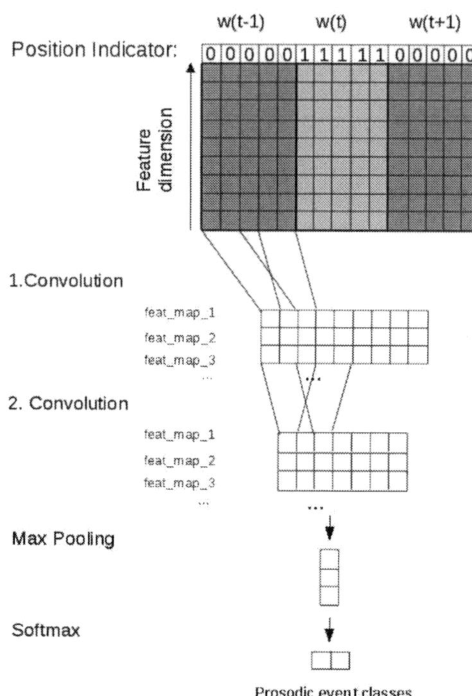

Figure 1: CNN for prosodic event recognition with an input window of 3 successive words and position indicating features.

text by indicating which frames belong to the current word or the neighbouring words.

We apply two convolution layers in order to expand the input information and then use max pooling to find the most salient features. In the first convolution layer we ensure that the filters always span all feature dimensions. All resulting feature maps are concatenated to one feature vector which is fed into the two-unit softmax layer.

4.2 Predicting prosodic labels on DIRNDL

We predict prosodic events for the whole DIRNDL subcorpus used in this paper. To simulate an application setting, we train the CNN model on a different dataset. Since the acoustic correlates of prosodic events as well as the connection between sentence prosody and information status exploited in this paper are similar in English and German, we train the prosodic event detector on English data and apply the model to the German DIRNDL corpus[5]. The data used to train the model is a 2.5 hour subset of the Boston University Radio

News Corpus (Ostendorf et al., 1995) that contains speech from 3 female and 2 male speakers and that includes manually labelled pitch accents and intonational phrase boundary tones. Hence, both corpora consist of read speech by radio news anchors. The prediction accuracy on the DIRNDL anaphora corpus is 81.9% for pitch accents and 85.5% for intonational phrase boundary tones[6]. The speaker-independent performance of this model on the Boston dataset is 83.5% accuracy for pitch accent detection and 89% for phrase boundary detection. We conclude that the prosodic event detector generalises well to the DIRNDL dataset and the obtained accuracies are appropriate for our experiments.

5 Coreference resolution

In this section, we describe the coreference resolver used in our experiments and how it was applied to create the baseline system using only automatic annotations.

5.1 IMS HotCoref DE

The IMS HotCoref DE coreference resolver is a state-of-the-art tool for German[7] (Rösiger and Kuhn, 2016). It is data-driven, i.e. it learns from annotated data with the help of pre-defined features using a structured perceptron that models coreference within a document as a directed tree. This way, it can exploit the tree structure to create non-local features (features that go beyond a pair of NPs). The standard features are text-based and consist mainly of string matching, part of speech, constituent parses, morphological information and combinations thereof.

5.2 Coreference resolution using automatic preprocessing

As we aim at coreference resolution applicable to new texts, all annotations used to create the text-based features are automatically predicted using NLP tools. It is frequently observed that the performance drops when the feature set is derived in this manner compared to using features based on manual annotations. For example, the performance of IMS HotCoref DE drops from 63.61

---

[6]The per-class accuracy is 82.1% for pitch accents and 37.1% for phrase boundaries. Despite these low quality phrase boundary annotations, we believe that, as a first step, their effectiveness can still be tested. This issue will be addressed in future work.

[7]www.ims.uni-stuttgart.de/forschung/ressourcen/werkzeuge/HOTCorefDe.html

to 48.61 CoNLL score[8] on the reference dataset
TüBA-9 D/Z. The system, pre-trained on TüBA,
yields a CoNLL score of 37.04 on DIRNDL with
predicted annotations. This comparatively low
score also confirms the assumption that the performance of a system trained on written text drops
when applied to spoken text. The drop in performance can also be explained by the slightly different domains (newspaper text and radio news).
However, if we train on the concatenation of the
train and development set of DIRNDL we achieve
a score of 46.11. This will serve as a baseline in
the following experiments.

6 Experiments

We test our prosodic features by adding them to
the feature set used in the baseline. We define
short NPs to be of length 3 or shorter[9]. In this
setup, we apply the feature only to short NPs. In
the *all NP* setting, the feature is used for all NPs.
The ratio of short vs. longer NPs in DIRNDL is
roughly 3:1. Note that we evaluate on the whole
test set in both cases. We report how the performance of the coreference resolver is affected in
three settings:

(a) trained and tested
on manual prosodic labels (short *gold*),

(b) trained on manual prosodic labels, but tested
on automatic labels (this simulates an application scenario where a pre-trained model is
applied to new texts (short *gold/auto*) and

(c) trained and tested on
automatic prosodic labels (short *auto*).

Table 1 shows the effect of the pitch accent presence feature on our data. All features perform significantly better than the baseline[10]. As expected,
the numbers are higher if we limit this feature to
short NPs. We believe that this is due to the fact
that the feature contributes most when it is most
meaningful: on short NPs, a pitch accent makes
it more likely for the NP to contain new information, whereas long NPs almost always have at

---

[8]We report the performance of the coreference system in
terms of the CoNLL score, the standard measure to assess the
quality of coreference resolution.

[9]In our experiments, this performed even better than
length 4 or shorter as used in Rösiger and Riester (2015).

[10]We compute significance using the Wilcoxon signed rank
test (Siegel and Castellan, 1988) at the 0.01 level.

Baseline	46.11	
+ Accent	short NPs	all NPs
+ Presence gold	53.99	49.68
+ Presence gold/auto	52.63	50.08
+ Presence auto	49.13	49.01

Table 1: Pitch accent presence

Baseline	46.11	
+ Nuclear accent	short NPs	all NPs
+ Presence gold	48.63	52.12
+ Presence gold/auto	48.46	51.45
+ Presence auto	48.01	50.64

Table 2: Nuclear accent presence

least one pitch accent, regardless of its information status. We achieve the highest performance
with gold labels, followed by the *gold/auto* version with a score that is not significantly worse
than the *gold* version. This is important for applications as it suggests that the loss in performance
is small when training on gold data and testing
on predicted data. As expected, the version that
is trained and tested on predicted data performs
worse, but is still significantly better than the baseline. Hence, prosodic information is helpful in all
three settings. It also shows that the assumption
on short NPs in the pilot study is also true for automatic labels.

Table 2 shows the effect of adding nuclear accent presence as a feature to the baseline. Again,
we report results that are all significantly better
than the baseline. The improvement is largest
when we apply the feature to all NPs, i.e. also
including long, complex NPs. This is in line with
the findings in the pilot study for long NPs. If we
restrict ourselves to just nuclear accents, this feature will receive the value *true* for only a few of
the short NPs that would otherwise have been assigned *true* in terms of general pitch accent presence. Therefore, nuclear pitch accents do not provide sufficient information for a majority of the
short NPs. For long NPs, however, the presence
of a nuclear accent is more meaningful.

The performance of the different systems follows the pattern present for pitch accent type: *gold*
> *gold/auto* > *auto*. Again, automatic prosodic
information contributes to the system's performance. The highest score when using automatic
labels is 50.64, as compared to 53.99 with gold
labels. To the best of our knowledge, these are
the best results reported on the DIRNDL anaphora
dataset so far.

EXPERTEN {der Großen KOALITION}₁ haben sich auf [...] ein Niedriglohn-
Experts *(of) the grand coalition* *have* *themselves* *on* *a* *low wage*

Konzept VERSTÄNDIGT. Die strittigen Themen [...] sollten bei der nächsten
concept *agreed.* *The controversial topics* *shall* *at* *the* *next*

Spitzenrunde **{der Koalition}₁** ANGESPROCHEN werden.
meeting *(of) the coalition* *raised* *be.*

*EN: Experts within the the grand coalition have agreed on a strategy to address [problems associated with] low income. At the next meeting, **the coalition** will talk about the controversial issues.*

Figure 2: Example from the DIRNDL dataset with English translation. The candidate NP (anaphor) of the coreference chain in question is marked in boldface, the antecedent is underlined. Pitch accented words are capitalised.

7 Analysis

In the following section, we discuss two examples from the DIRNDL dataset that provide some insight as to how the prosodic features helped coreference resolution in our experiments.

The first example is shown in Figure 2. The coreference chain marked in this example was not predicted by the baseline version. With prosodic information, however, the fact that the NP *"der Koalition"* is deaccented helped the resolver to recognise that this was given information: it refers to the recently introduced antecedent *"der Großen Koalition"*. This effect clearly supports our assumption that the absence of pitch accents helps for short NPs.

An additional effect of adding prosodic information that we observed concerns the length of antecedents determined by the resolver. In several cases, e.g. in Example (3), the baseline system incorrectly chose an embedded NP (1A) as the antecedent for a pronoun. The system with access to prosodic information correctly chose the longer NP (1B)[11]. Our analysis confirms that this is due to the accent on the short NP (on *Phelps*). The presence or absence of a pitch accent on the adjunct NP (on *USA*) does not appear to have an impact.

(3)   {{Michael PHELPS}₁ₐ aus den USA}₁в.
      {**Er**}₁ ...
      Michael Phelps from the USA. He ...

---

[11]The TüBA-D/Z guidelines state that the maximal extension of the NP should be chosen as the markable.
`http://www.sfs.uni-tuebingen.de/`
`fileadmin/static/ascl/resources/`
`tuebadz-coreference-manual-2007.pdf`

8 Conclusion and future work

We show that using prosodic labels that have been obtained automatically significantly improves the performance of a coreference resolver. In this work, we predict these labels using a CNN model and use these as additional features in IMS Hot-Coref DE, a coreference resolution system for German. Despite the quality of the predicted labels being slightly lower than the gold labels, we are still able to replicate results observed when using manually annotated prosodic information. This encouraging result also confirms that not only is prosodic information helpful to coreference resolution, but that it also has a positive effect even when predicted by a system.

A brief analysis of the resolver's output illustrates the effect of deaccentuation. Further work is necessary to investigate the impact on the length of the predicted antecedent.

One possibility to increase the quality of the predicted prosody labels would be to include the available lexico-syntactic information into the prosodic event detection model, since this has been shown to improve prosodic event recognition (Sun, 2002; Ananthakrishnan and Narayanan, 2008). To pursue coreference resolution directly on speech, a future step would be to perform all necessary annotations on automatic speech recognition output. As a first step, our results on German spoken text are promising and we expect them to be generalisable to other languages with similar prosody.

Acknowledgements

We would like to thank Kerstin Eckart for her help with the preparation of DIRNDL data. This work was funded by the German Science Foundation (DFG), Sonderforschungsbereich 732, Project A6 and A8, at the University of Stuttgart.

References

Marilisa Amoia, Kerstin Kunz, and Ekaterina Lapshinova-Koltunski. 2012. Coreference in spoken vs. written texts: a corpus-based analysis. In *Proceedings of LREC*.

Sankaranarayanan Ananthakrishnan and Shrikanth S. Narayanan. 2008. Automatic prosodic event detection using acoustic, lexical and syntactic evidence. In *IEEE Transactions on Audio, Speech and Language Processing*. volume 16, pages 216–228.

Stefan Baumann and Arndt Riester. 2013. Coreference, lexical givenness and prosody in German. *Lingua* 136:16–37.

Stefan Baumann and Anna Roth. 2014. Prominence and coreference – On the perceptual relevance of F0 movement, duration and intensity. In *Proceedings of Speech Prosody*. pages 227–231.

Anders Björkelund, Kerstin Eckart, Arndt Riester, Nadja Schauffler, and Katrin Schweitzer. 2014. The extended DIRNDL corpus as a resource for automatic coreference and bridging resolution. In *Proceedings of LREC*. pages 3222–3228.

Kerstin Eckart, Arndt Riester, and Katrin Schweitzer. 2012. A discourse information radio news database for linguistic analysis. In Sebastian Nordhoff Christian Chiarcos and Sebastian Hellmann, editors, *Linked Data in Linguistics: Representing and Connecting Language Data and Language Metadata*, Springer, pages 65–76.

Florian Eyben, Felix Weninger, Florian Groß, and Björn Schuller. 2013. Recent developments in openSMILE, the Munich open-source multimedia feature extractor. In *Proceedings of the 21st ACM international conference on Multimedia*. pages 835–838.

Mari Ostendorf, Patti Price, and Stefanie Shattuck-Hufnagel. 1995. The Boston University Radio News Corpus. Technical Report ECS-95-001, Boston University.

Sameer Pradhan, Alessandro Moschitti, Nianwen Xue, Olga Uryupina, and Yuchen Zhang. 2012. Conll-2012 shared task: Modeling multilingual unrestricted coreference in ontonotes. In *Joint Conference on EMNLP and CoNLL-Shared Task*. Association for Computational Linguistics, pages 1–40.

Marta Recasens, Lluís Màrquez, Emili Sapena, M. Antònia Martí, Mariona Taulé, Véronique Hoste, Massimo Poesio, and Yannick Versley. 2010. Semeval-2010 task 1: Coreference resolution in multiple languages. In *Proceedings of the 5th International Workshop on Semantic Evaluation*. Stroudsburg, PA, USA, SemEval '10, pages 1–8.

Andrew Rosenberg, Erica Cooper, Rivka Levitan, and Julia Hirschberg. 2012. Cross-language prominence detection. In *Speech Prosody*.

Ina Rösiger and Jonas Kuhn. 2016. IMS HotCoref DE: a data-driven co-reference resolver for German. In *Proceedings of LREC 2016*.

Ina Rösiger and Arndt Riester. 2015. Using prosodic annotations to improve coreference resolution of spoken text. In *Proceedings of ACL-IJCNLP*. pages 83–88.

Sidney Siegel and N. John Jr. Castellan. 1988. *Nonparametric Statistics for the Behavioral Sciences*. McGraw-Hill, Berkeley, CA, 2nd edition.

Sabrina Stehwien and Ngoc Thang Vu. 2017. Prosodic event detection using convolutional neural networks with context information. In *Proceedings of Interspeech*.

Michael Strube and Christoph Müller. 2003. A machine learning approach to pronoun resolution in spoken dialogue. In *Proceedings of the 41st Annual Meeting on Association for Computational Linguistics*. pages 168–175.

Xuejing Sun. 2002. Pitch accent prediction using ensemble machine learning. In *Proceedings of ICSLP-2002*. pages 16–20.

Jacques Terken and Julia Hirschberg. 1994. Deaccentuation of words representing 'given' information: Effects of persistence of grammatical function and surface position. *Language and Speech* 37(2):125–145.

Joel Tetreault and James Allen. 2004. Dialogue structure and pronoun resolution. In *Proceedings of the 5th Discourse Anaphora and Anaphor Resolution Colloquium*.

Carla Umbach. 2002. (De)accenting definite descriptions. *Theoretical Linguistics* 2/3:251–280.

Author Index

Association for Computational Linguistics
209 N. Eighth Street
Stroudsburg, Pennsylvania 18360

ISBN 978-1-5108-4762-0

CURRAN ASSOCIATES INC.
proceedings
.com